From Your Friends At **The MAILBOX** S0-BXN-939

SEPTEMBER

A MONTH OF IDEAS AT YOUR FINGERTIPS!

GRADES 4–6

SUNDER

WRITTEN BY

Becky Andrews, Irving P. Crump, Beth Gress,
Peggy W. Hambright, Paula Holdren, Simone Lepine,
Christine A. Thuman, Lynn Tutterow

EDITED BY

Becky Andrews, Lynn Bemer Coble,
Jennifer Rudisill, Gina Sutphin

ILLUSTRATED BY

Jennifer Tipton Bennett, Pam Crane, Teresa Davidson,
Sheila Krill, Rebecca Saunders, Barry Slate,
Donna K. Teal

COVER ART BY

Jennifer Tipton Bennett

©1996 by THE EDUCATION CENTER, INC.
All rights reserved.

ISBN# 1-56234-127-8

Manufactured in the United States
10 9 8 7 6 5 4 3

TABLE OF CONTENTS

September Calendar

School Begins

Sometime around the first of September, children around the world are beginning school. But in Australia, the new school year begins in late January, while in Chile school starts in March. Children in Japan begin the new school year in April. How would the school calendar be different if your students could plan it? Invite each student to create a new school calendar. Tell students how many instructional days there must be in the year; then let them take it from there!

Labor Day

The first Labor Day parade was held on September 5, 1882, in New York City. Since so many people participated in the events on that day, officials decided to honor workers every year. On June 28, 1894, President Grover Cleveland officially proclaimed the first Monday in September as Labor Day. Have students list what they think are the five most important jobs, giving at least two reasons for each choice. Compile the data into a class pictograph. For more Labor Day activities, see pages 26–33.

6—Birthday Of Jane Addams

Jane Addams—born on this day in 1860—worked for peace, social welfare, and women's rights. In 1889 she helped found Hull House, a community center for poor people in Chicago. For her humanitarian work, Addams was awarded the Nobel Peace Prize in 1931. Ask students what they think the word *humanitarian* means; then have them describe humanitarians in their own communities, churches, synagogues, etc. What special qualities do these people possess?

8—International Literacy Day

The United Nations sponsors International Literacy Day as a special day to celebrate and promote reading and writing. Share with your students the surprising fact that more than 25 percent of the adults in the world today can't read or write. To help students better understand this number, have 1/4 of them stand. Or tell students to think about four classes in your school—and to imagine that one entire class of students cannot read or write.

13—Roald Dahl's Birthday

Charlie And The Chocolate Factory, James And The Giant Peach, The BFG, Matilda, Danny: The Champion Of The World—what intermediate reader has not enjoyed one of Roald Dahl's offbeat novels? Dahl was born on this day in 1916 in Llandaff, Wales, England. Have each student write a brief paragraph about her favorite Roald Dahl character. Instruct the student to describe what she likes about that character and what she and the character have in common.

14—National Anthem Day

"The Star-Spangled Banner" was written by Francis Scott Key during the War of 1812. Aboard an enemy ship, Key watched as the British bombarded Fort McHenry. The next morning—overjoyed to see that "our flag was still there"—he wrote a poem. Key later put the words of his poem with the tune of an English drinking song. Does your school have a school song? If not, challenge your students to create one. Instruct each student to write two verses and a chorus; then have him decide on a tune for the lyrics. Hold auditions, and have students choose their favorite song from among their classmates' entries.

16—Pilgrims Set Sail

On this day in 1620, the Pilgrims set sail on the *Mayflower* from Plymouth, England. On board were 95 adults, 32 children, and 2 dogs. What was life like for the Pilgrim children in this new land? What special challenges did they face? What did they do for fun? Share *Eating The Plates: A Pilgrim Book Of Food And Manners* by Lucille Recht Penner (Scholastic Inc., 1991) with your students. Have them compare and contrast the everyday lives of the Pilgrim children with their present-day lives.

19—Mickey Mouse's Debut

On September 19, 1928, Mickey Mouse was introduced to the world in a cartoon titled *Steamboat Willie*. This film was the first cartoon to use sound. Ask students to describe their favorite cartoon characters. Were any of these characters created by The Walt Disney Company? Challenge students to create new cartoon characters for Disney to feature in its next film.

25—Establishment Of Yosemite National Park

One of America's most breathtaking parks, Yosemite, was established on this day in 1890. Visitors to Yosemite can see the highest waterfall in the United States, hike through Yosemite Valley, and admire majestic redwood trees. Is it important for our nation to maintain and support national parks? Have students write about whether they think our national parks are important.

National Dog Week

National Dog Week begins on the Sunday of the last full week in September. Begin a dog information board that includes facts about man's best friend. Have students research such questions as: "Why do dogs pant? Why does a dog wag its tail? Why does a dog turn around and around before it lies down? Can a dog see colors?" Post index cards with students' information on the display along with photos of your students' dogs.

Why do dogs pant?
Dogs don't sweat like humans. As a dog pants, evaporation of water from the mouth cools its body.

Can a dog see colors?
Dogs are color blind. They can tell colors apart only by recognizing various shades of gray.

Teacher's September Resource Calendar

   ## A Handy List Of Special Days

 The early Roman calendar began with March. So September was its seventh month. *Septem* is Latin for "seven."

 Labor Day is the first Monday in September.

 2 In 1789 Congress established the U.S. Treasury Department.

4 The first roll-film camera, registered as Kodak, was patented by George Eastman in 1888.

 7 The nickname Uncle Sam was first used in *The Troy Post* of Troy, New York, in 1813.

 8 The first permanent settlement of Europeans on the North American continent was established at St. Augustine, Florida, in 1565.

 9 On this day in 1776, the Second Continental Congress ruled that the "United Colonies" would from this day forward be referred to as the "United States."

11 Henry Hudson discovered Manhattan Island on this day in 1609.

 18 George Washington laid the cornerstone of the Capitol in Washington, DC, in 1793.

 19 Abraham Lincoln delivered his Gettysburg Address on this day in 1863.

 20 On this day in 1519, Portuguese explorer Ferdinand Magellan—with five ships and 270 men—set sail on the first voyage around the world.

 26 On this day in 1774, folk hero John Chapman—nicknamed Johnny Appleseed— was born in Leominster, Massachusetts.

 28 Teachers' Day is a national holiday in Taiwan. It honors Confucius, who was born on this day in 551 B.C.

  29 The United States established a Regular Army of 700 men on this day in 1789.

30 Babe Ruth hit his 60th home run of the season for the New York Yankees on this day in 1927.

September Clip Art

Use on the following items:

- letters to parents
- games
- nametags
- notes to students
- homework assignments
- newsletters
- awards
- learning centers
- bulletin boards

CLASSROOM TIMES

Teacher: _____   Date: _____

SEPTEMBER

Highlights

Don't Forget!

Hats Off To...

Special Events

Help Wanted

FREE-TIME FUN for September!

Tackle these 20 terrific tasks when you finish your work.

Monday	Tuesday	Wednesday	Thursday	Friday
Labor Day (the first Monday in September) honors working people. List five workers who helped you last week. How did each worker help you?	Without looking at one, describe what is printed on a one-dollar bill.	What's your favorite fast-food restaurant? Describe it. List three suggestions for making it better.	Describe the last neighborly thing you did.	Letter a sheet of paper from A–Z. List a cartoon character that begins with each letter.
September is the ninth month of the year. How old will you be on 9-9-1999? **9 9 9**	List ten different definitions for the word *set*. Use a dictionary if you need help. **set**	Count the e's in this box. Then make an estimate for the entire page. Check your estimate. 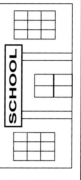	Do you think that CDs should be rated (G, PG, R, etc.) like movies? Why or why not?	Use the words *to, too,* and *two* all in the same sentence. *to two too*
Make a list of ten creative ways you could use a brick.	List the letters in *September* in a column. Write a fun fall activity that begins with each letter. Soccer games Eating pumpkin pie Playing with friends	You're on stage! Write a description telling how you'll entertain the audience.	From memory, draw the front of your school. 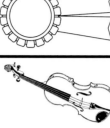 SCHOOL	*Smog* (smoke + fog) and *motel* (motor + hotel) are *portmanteaus*—words formed by combining two words. Create five new portmanteaus. MOTEL
Make a list of ten homophone pairs. One word in each pair must be a proper noun. *Maine & mane* 	Choose a six-letter word. Make a pyramid like this one. a pa lap pale lapse please	Make a pictograph that shows the kinds of shoes your classmates are wearing today.	Letter a sheet of paper from A–Z. For each letter of the alphabet, write a word that has double letters. *aardvark rubble accent fiddle* 	What was the highlight of this month for you? Write a description of this special event.

8

©1996 The Education Center, Inc. • SEPTEMBER • TEC198

Note To The Teacher: Have each student staple a copy of this page inside a file folder. Direct students to store their completed work inside their folders.

Desktag: Duplicate student copies on construction paper. Have each student personalize and decorate his pattern; then laminate the patterns and use them as desktags during September.

Award: Duplicate multiple copies. Keep them handy at your desk along with a supply of new pencils. If desired, tape a new pencil to the back of each award after you've filled it out.

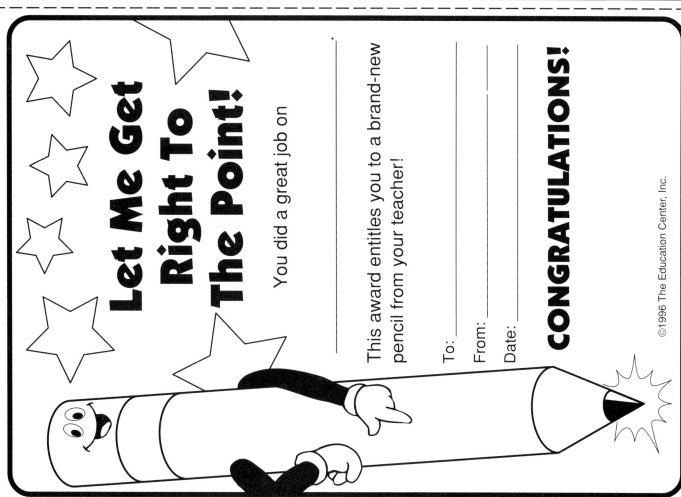

Let Me Get Right To The Point!

You did a great job on _____

This award entitles you to a brand-new pencil from your teacher!

To: _____

From: _____

Date: _____

CONGRATULATIONS!

©1996 The Education Center, Inc.

YAHOO IT'S A NEW YEAR!

It's back-to-school time, and you're ready to take the bull by the horns and plan a ripsnortin' successful year! How do you get started on the right foot? A great place to begin is this collection of back-to-school bulletin boards, activities, tips, and reproducibles. With these teaching tools in your saddlebags, you can bet your bottom dollar it'll be a rootin'-tootin' terrific year!

A Rootin'-Tootin' Welcome!

Say howdy to your new class with a bulletin-board display that doubles as a back-to-school discussion starter. Enlarge and color the cowpoke pattern on page 19; then mount it on a bulletin board. Add the speech bubble as shown. Duplicate the sheriff's badge pattern (one per student) on page 24 on yellow paper. After cutting out the badges, label them with student names and mount them with pushpins on the board. On the first day, give each child a copy of the reproducible on page 20. Have each student answer the questions; then have her attach her paper to the board, pinning her badge to a corner of the paper. During the first week, discuss the suggestions on the sheets with the class. Use this discussion to lead into a session during which you and your new students establish classroom rules and goals for the year.

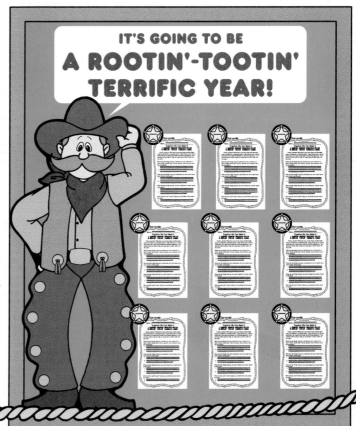

First-Day Tickets

Here's an idea that guarantees a ripsnortin' successful first day! A week before school begins, send each student a short, personal note welcoming her to your class. Inside the note, insert a copy of the first-day ticket on page 19. Instruct the student that she will need to bring the ticket to school on the first day to gain admittance into your class.

On the first day, have students deposit their tickets in a cowboy hat or other container as they enter the room. (Be sure to have extra tickets on hand for students who forget theirs.) As you progress through the day, periodically stop and draw a ticket from the hat. Reward the student whose name is on the ticket with a small treat, such as a new pencil, an inexpensive set of markers, or another school supply. Continue drawing names throughout the day until every student has won a prize.

Howdy, Helpers!

Round up a posse of hardworking helpers with an easy-to-make-and-manage display. Duplicate the "WANTED" poster on page 22 on light brown paper (one per classroom job). Label each poster with a job; then laminate the posters. Cut a slit on the dotted line on each poster and insert a paper clip. Mount the posters on a bulletin board along with an enlarged copy of the cowpoke on page 19. Before the first day, collect a cowboy hat, a bandana, and a solid-colored vest. Make a tagboard mustache as well.

On the first day, ask each student to don the hat, bandana, and vest. Place a small roll of tape on the back of the mustache; then have the student stick the mustache on his (or her!) face and strike a cowboy pose while you take a photo of him. (Be sure the photos are horizontal, not vertical, shots. Also change the roll of tape on the mustache after each photo.) After the pictures are developed, put a self-sticking label on each photo. Have each student write a cowboy name for himself or herself, such as Deadeye Davey or Quickdraw Quincy, on the label. Collect the photos and store them in an envelope attached to the board. Assign jobs each week by clipping the students' photos to the posters.

Bulletin Boards Without The Bother

The start of a new school year is busy enough without having to labor over bulletin boards. Use these quick tips to create dazzling displays without the bother:

- Add pizzazz to a plain bulletin board by placing self-sticking metallic stars on the background paper.
- For an eye-catching way to display students' work, mount artwork or favorite papers on solid-colored, paper placemats.
- Need more display space? Make a mini bulletin board by laminating a large piece of colorful poster board. Transparent or masking tape will adhere any object—from student papers to seasonal cutouts—to the poster.
- Make a stunning border in a jiffy by mounting two-inch-wide ribbon—solid colored, striped, or any design—around the edges of your board.

Lookin' Ahead!

Give your new students a sneak peek at the year ahead with this fun display! Enlarge the steer pattern on page 22; then make three copies to color, cut out, and staple to the bottom of a board as shown. Add the title "Have You 'Herd' About ___ Grade?" Directly on the background paper, use brightly colored markers to list items that students can look forward to in the coming year—new skills they will acquire, units they'll study, field trips, etc. After seeing this display, your students will be thrilled they've "moooved" up a grade!

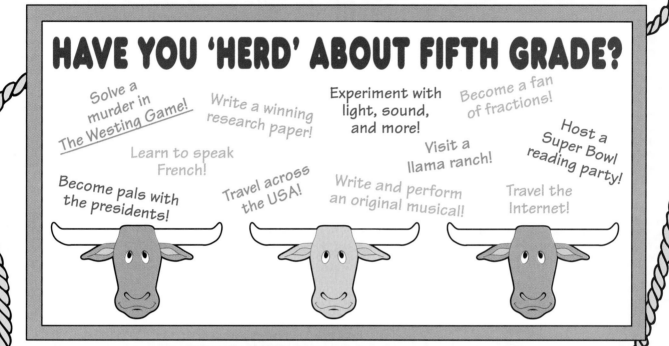

Birthday Bonanza

There's no doubt about it—intermediate kids still get a kick out of celebrating their birthdays! To make a birthday display that is maintained by students (instead of you), duplicate the small boot patterns on page 24 (one per child). Instruct each student to write his name and birthdate on his boot, color it with crayons or markers, and then cut it out. Have two students glue the boots around the edges of a large piece of poster board as shown. Label the poster with the title "Kick Up Your Heels—It's Your Birthday!"; then laminate it.

Each month assign a cooperative group to be in charge of updating the birthday poster. On a child's birthday, the group in charge writes the honored student's name and birthdate on the poster with a wipe-off marker. After a rousing rendition of "Happy Birthday," ask one student from the group to pass around a construction-paper copy of the boot pattern on page 21. Have each student write a compliment about the birthday child on the boot before passing it to the next classmate. Clip a copy of the no-homework coupon on page 19 to the boot before giving it to the child to take home.

Sit A Spell And Read

Try these ideas to create a reading center that invites book lovers to sit a spell and read:

- To extend a western theme, sew four bandanas together as shown. Make several of these large squares. Stitch two of the squares together, leaving a small opening for stuffing with fiberfill. Hand-stitch the opening closed, and you've got a soft, colorful pillow for your reading center.

- Have each student bring an old, clean T-shirt to class. Let students decorate their shirts with fabric paint; then have a parent volunteer sew up the neck opening, one sleeve opening, and the bottom of each shirt. Show each student how to stuff her shirt with fiberfill through the unsewn sleeve opening. Then show students how to hand-stitch the opening shut. There you have it—comfortable pillows that will suit your students to a "tee"!

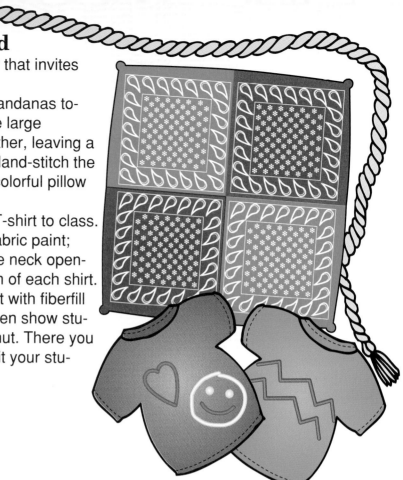

Say Howdy To The Head Honcho

Introduce yourself to your new cowpokes with an eye-catching teacher feature. Use a small bulletin board or other display area in the classroom. In the display, include the following items that focus on you, the "new teacher": family photos, diplomas, awards that you've earned, an elementary-grade report card, a picture of yourself when you were in the same grade that you're currently teaching, plus items that represent some of your favorite sports, hobbies, and pastimes. During the first week of school, take time to share these items with your students. It's one way of letting your students know that you're a person outside the classroom too!

Say Howdy To Each Other

More than likely, you'll have students in your class who are new to the community and school. A scavenger-hunt activity is the perfect icebreaker for students on the first day back to school. Duplicate page 23 for each student. Instruct students to circulate about the classroom seeking their classmates' signatures to fill the boxes. (A student should not sign his or her name more than twice in any vertical, horizontal, or diagonal row.) Challenge students to completely fill their grids with signatures. After a predetermined amount of time, have students return to their seats. Follow up this activity with the graphing lessons on page 14.

Say, pardner— how many brothers and sisters do you have?

First-Day Graphs

Use the information that your students gathered in the "Say Howdy To Each Other" scavenger hunt on page 13 to complete each of the following graphing activities:

- Ask each student whose first and last names begin with the same letter to raise her hand. Then ask how many total students are in the class. Finally ask students how they would show such information in a circle graph. Determine the two criteria for the graph: students whose first and last names begin with the same letter and students whose names begin with different letters. After counting how many students fit in each category, have each student make a circle graph to show that information. When everyone is finished, draw a large circle on the chalkboard and invite a volunteer to illustrate his graph in the circle.

- Use the information about students' hobbies gathered in the scavenger hunt to create a class pictograph. List all of the students' hobbies on the chalkboard, including ones not listed on the reproducible scavenger hunt. Then use tally marks to show the number of students who enjoy each hobby. Ask students to suggest symbols to represent the different hobbies. Then have each student create a pictograph. When everyone is finished, ask a volunteer to draw his pictograph on the chalkboard.

- Expand the information about students who ride their bikes to school. List the different ways that students get to school: by car, school bus, bicycle, walking, and any other categories. Poll students one at a time and make a tally mark beside one of the categories for each student. Then instruct students to make bar graphs that show the information.

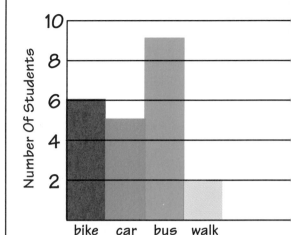

How Students Get To School

Parent Photo Notes

Give your new students' parents an up close and personal look at your class every time you send a note home. During the first weeks of school, take a roll or two of photographs showing students engaged in a variety of classroom activities. After having the film developed, ask a photo shop to transform the pictures into photo cards similar to those sent by many families at Christmas. Jot notes home to parents on the blank portion of the cards. When you want to send a note home, you'll not only be keeping the lines of communication open, but you'll also be treating the parent to a photo of your class in action. Take new photos as the year progresses and order new cards periodically.

Dear Mrs. Gonzalez,
Luis has made wonderful progress with his multiplication facts. He passed the last timed test with flying colors!
Mrs. Krieg

Back-To-School Art Projects

Give your new buckaroos a chance to show off their artistic talents with the following creative art projects:

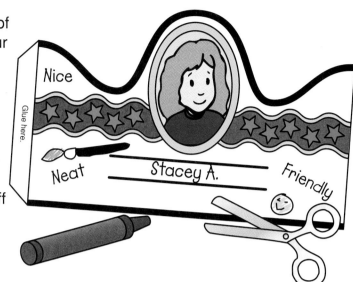

- **"Border-rific"!:** To create an eye-catching border for a bulletin board, duplicate a copy of page 25 for each student in your class. If your bulletin board is eight feet wide, then 12 patterns will be needed for each of the top and bottom borders. Have 12 students turn their patterns upside down when completing them—these patterns together will make up the top border. To complete a section of border, have students glue their patterns together at the tabs; then have students trim off any extra tabs.

- **This Class Really Stacks Up!:** Every student contributes to this back-to-school art project—a perfect centerpiece for your Open House. Collect six or seven boxes of varying sizes. Make sure that the boxes stack easily and that you have a box for every four students. Divide your students into groups of four and give each group a box. Instruct the students in each group to decorate the four sides of the box—one side per group member. Instruct each student to include a variety of illustrations on his section: drawings of family and pets; pictures cut from magazines that illustrate favorite hobbies, sports, and other pastimes; symbols that represent important events in the student's life; plus any other items that the student would like to display. When each group has completed its box, stack all of the boxes on top of each other. Hang a sign labeled "This Class Really Stacks Up!" from the ceiling right above the top box.

Fine-Thinkin' Flu

Reward students early in the year for using their noggins with this slightly silly—but motivating—idea. Fill an empty pill or vitamin bottle with jelly beans, M&M's®, Skittles®, or other small treats. Add a label to the bottle that reads "Rx: Take to relieve symptoms of the fine-thinkin' flu. One tablet as soon as symptoms appear." When a student exhibits good thinking skills or the perseverance to figure out a tough problem, walk over to the child's desk, put your hand on his forehead, and announce, "My goodness, I think you've got the fine-thinkin' flu. Better take care of that!" Then treat the student with a "pill" from the bottle. For students who show improvement in a particularly tough skill, fill another bottle with a different candy to take care of the "Better-Work Bug."

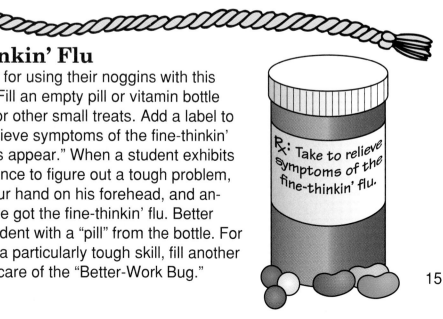

Back-To-School Centers In A Snap!

You want to prepare some terrific learning centers for the first weeks of school, but who has time? You do—when you use the following "centers-in-a-snap" ideas:

- **Class Diary:** For a center that results in a student-written journal of the year's activities, label a composition notebook "Wow, What A Day!" Write the date of each school day on the top of a page in the notebook to create a dated journal. During center or free time, encourage students to write on that day's page, telling about the most memorable event of the day or something new they've learned. At the end of the school year, you'll have a memory book that provides a day-by-day record of your class's activities.

Extra time on your hands? Here's an activity that's sure to TIDE you over!

- **Laundry-Box Centers:** Recycling used laundry boxes can give you portable centers that are sturdy, colorful, and versatile. Ask friends and colleagues to help you collect a variety of empty, cleaned laundry boxes (the kinds with plastic handles work best). In each box, place a variety of duplicated brainteasers, worksheets, flash cards, and other practice activities. Store an answer key inside each box for self-checking. On the back of each box, tape a large index card labeled with directions that include the name of the laundry soap brand. For example:

  — Extra time on your hands? Here's an activity that's sure to TIDE you over!
  — CHEER up! Here's a fun activity you can do next!
  — You'll GAIN extra-credit points by completing this activity!
  — Are you BOLD enough to accept this challenge? Give it a try!
  — WISK away the "what-do-I-do-now?" blues with this challenging activity!
  — DASH the doldrums away with this fun activity!

  Place all of the laundry-box centers on a table, on a windowsill, or along the floor under your chalkboard. Students can easily take the boxes back to their desks to complete the activities. These sturdy, boxed centers can also be sent home for practice with parents.

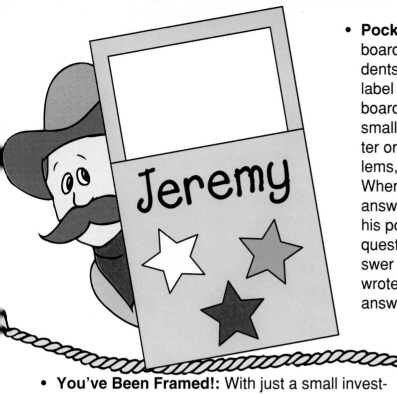

- **Pockets Full Of Puzzlers:** Turn a piece of poster board into an instant center that's stocked by your students. Give each child a library pocket to decorate and label with his name. Mount the pockets on the poster board. Add one or two extra pockets in which to store small index cards. Challenge students to use their center or free time to write review questions, math problems, or challenging brainteasers on the cards. When a student has written a question, he writes the answer on the back of the card, then inserts the card in his pocket. During free time, let a student pull a question from his pocket and challenge the class to answer it. Award extra-credit points to the student who wrote the question and the classmate who correctly answers it.

- **You've Been Framed!:** With just a small investment, you can make a collection of centers that can be changed in an instant. Purchase several inexpensive picture frames (look for plastic frames or frames that use thick acetate instead of glass). Inside each frame, insert a piece of paper on which you've written a challenge question, math problems, a story starter, or any other task. Or insert cut-out magazine pictures and have students write descriptions, dialogues, or math problems based on the photos. Place the frames on a windowsill, table, or chalktray. A student can take a frame back to her desk and complete the activity. To make the picture-frame centers self-checking, insert a sheet listing all the answer keys in one large frame. Keep this frame in a central location.

Solve these problems, then check using a calculator.

825 x 9 =
908 x 7 =
377 x 5 =
279 x 8 =

Which of these are things you would wear?

gimlet
derby
château
miter
cache

Make five lists about yourself. Try these ideas:
- 5 things I do really well
- 5 ways I help others
- 5 people I'll never forget
- 5 things that make me mad
- 5 words to describe me

① (50x2)+(18+12)=

② (15x3)-(6x5)+2=

- **The 60-Second Challenge:** Motivate students to practice their mental math with this easy center idea. Number a set of colored index cards; then label each card with a mental math problem such as the ones shown. Make an answer key as well. Store the cards in a large, zippered plastic bag. Place the answer key and a one-minute timer in a separate bag. Store both bags in a basket at a center. A student selects a card from the bag. Then he turns the timer over and tries to mentally solve the problem in 60 seconds or less. He checks his answer by using the answer key card.

Back In The Saddle

Your cowpokes' math skills may be a little rusty after summer vacation. Get them back in the saddle again with this collaborative game that reviews basic skills. First divide students into five groups and have each group elect a recorder to communicate his group's answers during the game. To begin play, roll a pair of dice three times. Announce each roll to the class; then write it on the chalkboard. The object of the game is for each group to list as many numbers and equations as possible that can be formed from combinations of the three numbers. Give the groups three minutes to come up with their answers as the recorder lists them. For example, rolls of 3, 7, and 9 could result in the following acceptable answers:

3	**73**	$3 \times 9 = $ **27**
7	**79**	$7 \times 9 = $ **63**
9	**93**	$(7 + 3) \times 9 = $ **90**
37	**97**	$(7 - 3) + 9 = $ **13**
39	$3 \times 7 = $ **21**	$(7 + 9) \times 3 = $ **48**

After calling time, score each group's efforts. If all five groups have a particular result—such as 21 in the above sample—each group earns one point. If four of the groups have the same result, each group earns two points. If three groups have the same answer, they each earn three points. If only two groups have a particular answer, each group is awarded four points. And if one group is the only one to come up with a particular answer, that group earns ten points. Play until a group reaches a predetermined number of points.

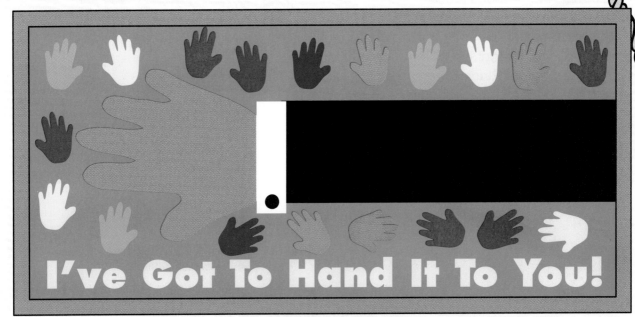

A Handy Display

For an easy-to-make motivational display, cut out a large sleeve and hand from bulletin-board paper; then mount them as the centerpiece for the display. Have students trace their hands on colorful sheets of construction paper and cut out the tracings. Attach a hand cutout to the board each time the class exhibits good behavior or manners during the school day. After students have earned a certain number of hands, treat them to a special snack or a video.

Use the cowpoke pattern with "A Rootin'-Tootin' Welcome!" on page 10 and "Howdy, Helpers!" on page 11.

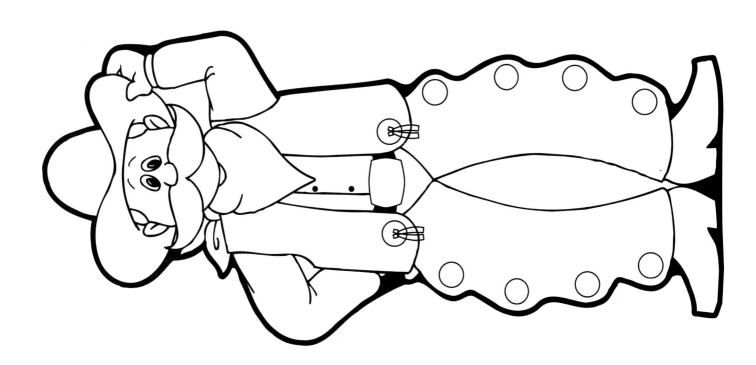

©1996 The Education Center, Inc. • *SEPTEMBER* • TEC198

Use the no-homework coupons with "Birthday Bonanza" on page 12. Use the tickets with "First-Day Tickets" on page 10.

ADMIT ONE

Back-To-School Buckaroo
to
_____'s _____ -Grade Class
on the first day of school.

Write your name here; then bring this ticket with you to school on the first day of class.

_____

ADMIT ONE

Back-To-School Buckaroo
to
_____'s _____ -Grade Class
on the first day of school.

Write your name here; then bring this ticket with you to school on the first day of class.

_____

GIVE HOMEWORK THE BOOT TONIGHT!

In honor of your birthday, take a night off from homework by skipping the following assignment: _____

Happy Birthday, Buckaroo!

To: _____
From: _____
Date: _____

GIVE HOMEWORK THE BOOT TONIGHT!

In honor of your birthday, take a night off from homework by skipping the following assignment: _____

Happy Birthday, Buckaroo!

To: _____
From: _____
Date: _____

Name _____

Together We Can Make It
A ROOTIN'-TOOTIN' TERRIFIC YEAR!

Howdy, pardner! Welcome to your new class and the beginning of a ripsnortin' successful year! To get things off to a sensational start, sit a spell and answer the following questions. Your answers will be used to help our class plan a rootin'-tootin' terrific year!

What are two things that your teacher can do to make this a rootin'-tootin' terrific year? (Sorry, pardner, but homework can't be eliminated!)

1. _____

2. _____

What are two things that your classmates can do to make this a rootin'-tootin' terrific year?

1. _____

2. _____

What are two things that you can do to make this a rootin'-tootin' terrific year?

1. _____

2. _____

What are two rootin'-tootin' topics you would like to learn about this year?

1. _____

2. _____

Name _____

Together We Can Make It
A ROOTIN'-TOOTIN' TERRIFIC YEAR!

Howdy, pardner! Welcome to your new class and the beginning of a ripsnortin' successful year! To get things off to a sensational start, sit a spell and answer the following questions. Your answers will be used to help our class plan a rootin'-tootin' terrific year!

What are two things that your teacher can do to make this a rootin'-tootin' terrific year? (Sorry, pardner, but homework can't be eliminated!)

1. _____

2. _____

What are two things that your classmates can do to make this a rootin'-tootin' terrific year?

1. _____

2. _____

What are two things that you can do to make this a rootin'-tootin' terrific year?

1. _____

2. _____

What are two rootin'-tootin' topics you would like to learn about this year?

1. _____

2. _____

©1996 The Education Center, Inc. • SEPTEMBER • TEC198

Note To The Teacher: Use these reproducibles with "A Rootin'-Tootin' Welcome!" on page 10.

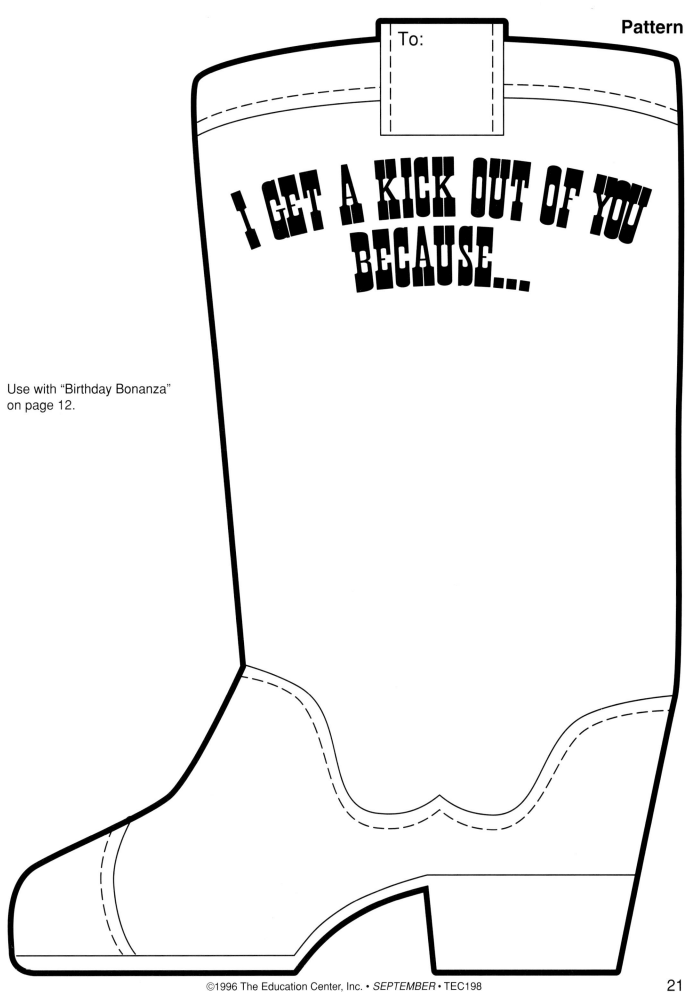

To:

I GET A KICK OUT OF YOU BECAUSE...

Use with "Birthday Bonanza" on page 12.

Patterns

Use the steer pattern with "Lookin' Ahead!" on page 12. Use the "WANTED" poster with "Howdy, Helpers!" on page 11.

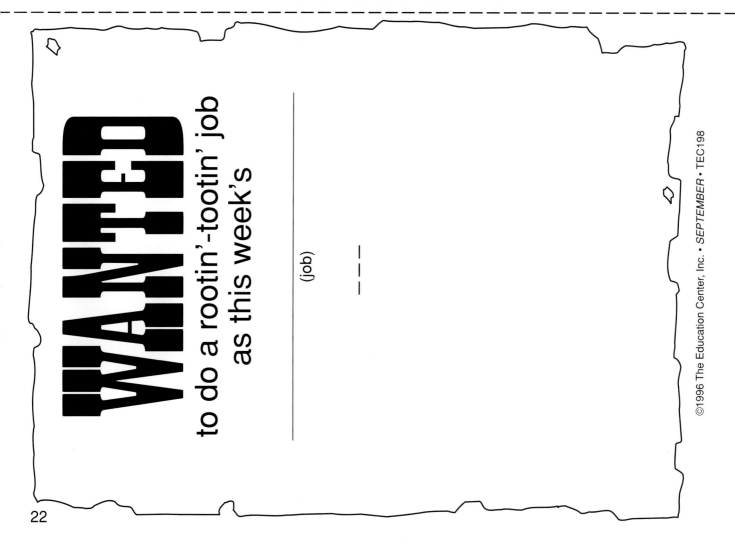

WANTED

to do a rootin'-tootin' job
as this week's

_____
(job)

Name _____

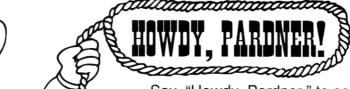

HOWDY, PARDNER!

Say, "Howdy, Pardner," to each of your classmates with this scavenger-hunt activity. Walk around the classroom and visit with the other students. Try to get a signature in each box of the grid. A student should not sign his or her name more than two times in any vertical, horizontal, or diagonal row.

_____'s first and last names begin with the same letter. *Suzie Smith*	_____ was born in another state.	_____ has visited a foreign country.	_____ is the youngest child in a family of three children.	_____ walks to school.
_____'s favorite food is pizza.	_____'s first name has more vowels than consonants. **Aimee**	_____ loves science fiction movies and books. A Wrinkle In Time	_____ has read ten or more R. L. Stine books. Goose-Bumps	_____ has ridden a camel or an elephant (a real one!).
_____ has an autograph of a famous person. *Cal Ripken, Jr.*	_____ has both an older brother and a younger brother.	_____ traveled somewhere by train this summer.	_____ loves to fish.	_____'s hobby is collecting coins (or stamps, baseball cards, etc.). RED SOX
_____ visited at least five states during the summer.	_____ loves to skate.	_____ attended a professional ball game during the past six months. Astros	_____ visited Walt Disney World® during the summer.	_____ can water-ski.
_____ earned all *A*'s during at least one grading term last year. Report Card	_____ knows how to cross-stitch. LOVE	_____ learned how to swim over the summer.	_____ rides his or her bike to school.	_____ has at least five pets.

Bonus Box: Count all of the squares in the grid above. How many do you see?

©1996 The Education Center, Inc. • *SEPTEMBER* • TEC198 • Key p. 95

Note To The Teacher: Use with "Say Howdy To Each Other" on page 13.

Patterns

Use the boot patterns with "Birthday Bonanza" on page 12. Use the badge patterns with "A Rootin'-Tootin' Welcome!" on page 10.

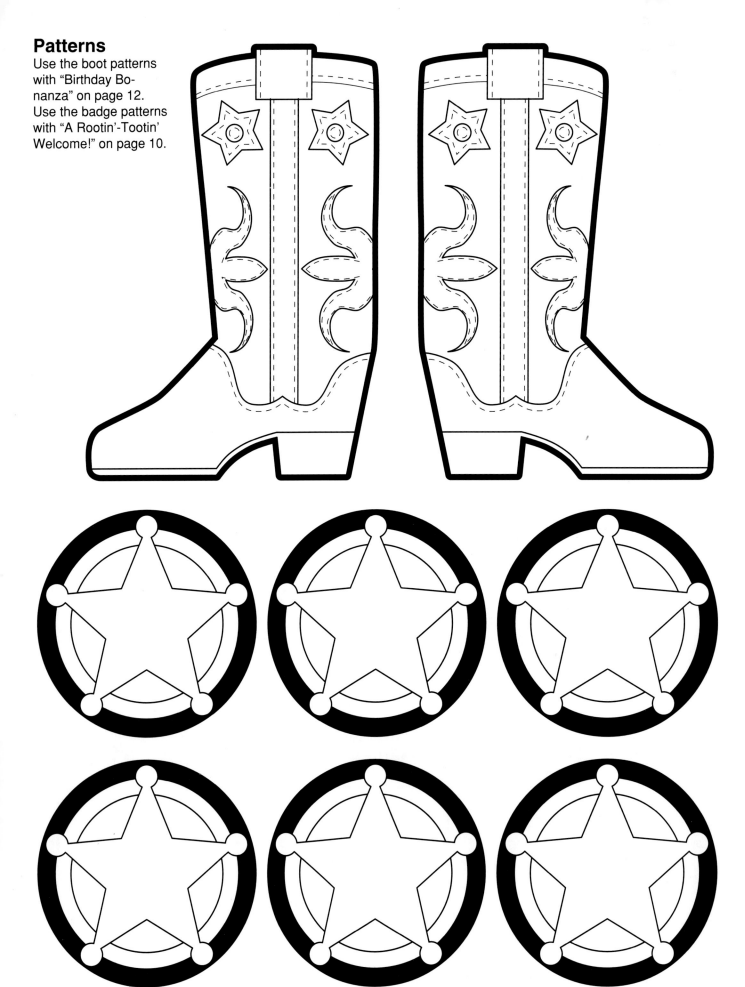

Name _____

"Border-rific"!

Directions:

1. Write your first name and the initial of your last name as neatly as possible between the two lines below.

2. Bring a school picture or any snapshot of yourself to class. Trim the picture so that it fits in the oval; then use rubber cement to keep it in place.

3. In the remaining blank areas of the pattern, draw symbols and write words that describe yourself. Include symbols that tell about your family, interests, hobbies, favorite sports, etc.

4. Color and decorate the rest of the pattern.

5. Cut out the pattern on the bold line and along the dotted line of the tab.

6. Give your pattern to your teacher, who will show you and your classmates how to glue the patterns together to make a bulletin-board border.

Glue here.

©1996 The Education Center, Inc. • SEPTEMBER • TEC198

Note To The Teacher: Use with "'Border-rific'!" on page 15. Provide students with scissors, rubber cement, glue, and markers or crayons. Several days before doing this activity, have students bring photos of themselves to class. If a student can't provide a photo, let him draw a self-portrait in the oval instead.

HATS OFF TO LABORERS!
Celebrating Labor Day With A Look At Careers

Each year we celebrate the contributions of our country's workers with the Labor Day holiday. Someday your students will be part of our country's labor force. Start your year off by helping students examine careers that might be a part of their futures.

A Labor Day Celebration

Throughout history hats have symbolized career roles. Introduce your Labor Day unit by holding a Hat Day. Brainstorm the different types of hats that people wear on their jobs. Some examples include a firefighter's helmet, a construction worker's hard hat, a nurse's cap, the netting worn by a food industry worker, or the cap of a police officer, airplane pilot, or ship's captain. Invite each student to bring a career-related hat (or a magazine picture of such a hat) to school for Hat Day. Use the hats as a springboard for discussing the reasons for various hat shapes, parts, and materials. For example, why does a miner's hat contain a flashlight? Why are people who work in commercial kitchens often required to wear hair nets? What useful functions are included in the design of a firefighter's helmet? By the end of the discussion, your students' heads will be filled to the brim with information—and more questions—about careers!

Don't Forget Your Hat!

Tip your hat to creativity by having students design hats for a variety of careers. Begin by brainstorming a list of careers that aren't usually associated with an identifiable hat. If needed use the "ABC Careers" listed on page 27 to get started. Have each student select two careers from the list and design a hat for each on scrap paper. After duplicating page 30 for each student, instruct each child to draw his final designs on the patterns; then have him add the name of the career and the career's description on each pattern. After students have cut out their patterns, display these beautiful bonnets on a bulletin board entitled "Don't Forget Your Hat!"

A Career Hat For: _Ornithologist_
Job Description: _A scientist who specializes in the study of birds_

Name: _Debbie S._

We Tip Our Hats To You!

Inspire students to consider a variety of careers by looking at the lifetime accomplishments of famous people. Instruct each student to read a biography or an autobiography about a famous person. Duplicate the contract "Hats Off To A Lifetime Of Achievement!" on page 31 for each student. Then have the student share her knowledge of that famous person and his career by completing the desired number of contracted activities. Set aside time for students to introduce their famous people to their classmates.

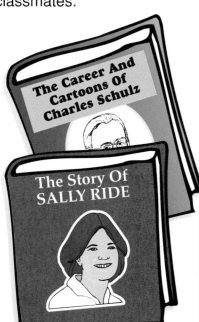

An ABC Career Exploration

Explore a variety of jobs by having students create an ABC book of careers. Assign one letter of the alphabet to each student. Give the student a colorful cutout of her letter and a contrasting sheet of light-colored paper. Instruct each student to research a career that begins with her letter (see the list on the right). Direct the student to glue her letter on the colored paper; then have her write the title of the career at the top of the page and illustrate the career. Finally have her write a job description of her career, a "One Day In The Life Of _____" short story about someone in this career, or an original poem describing the career. Staple the completed pages between two covers to make a class book.

ABC Careers

Accountant, anthropologist, archaeologist, architect
Baker, biologist, botanist
Cardiologist, cartographer, chef, chemist, conservationist
Dentist, dermatologist
Engineer, entomologist, environmentalist
Farmer, firefighter, forest ranger
Gardener, geologist
Hairdresser, helicopter pilot, horticulturist
Illustrator, inventor
Jockey, journalist, judge
Kindergarten teacher, karate instructor
Lawyer, lifeguard, lumberjack
Mathematician, musician
Naturalist, neurologist, nurse
Ornithologist, orthodontist
Physicist, pilot, police officer, psychologist
Quilter
Receptionist, reporter
Scientist, sheriff, sociologist
Teacher, truck driver
Undertaker, urologist
Valet, veterinarian
Waiter, welder, writer
X-ray technician (radiologist)
Yeoman, yoga instructor
Zookeeper, zoologist

Outstanding In Their Fields

For a cooperative research project, divide your class into groups of four. Using one of the career lists from "Don't Forget Your Hat!" on page 26 or "An ABC Career Exploration" on page 27, give each group seven to ten different careers to research. Instruct each group to use reference materials and trade books to identify the name of a famous person in each career field. Duplicate the pattern on page 32 for each student. Have the student select one name from her group's list and write a report about that person on the profile sheet. Direct her to include information on the person's career, what got the person interested in this career, and whether the person's career made him famous (as opposed to something else he accomplished). Have students cut out their completed reports to display on a bulletin board titled "Profiles Of Success."

Examples of career/person matches:
archaeologist—Howard Carter
conservationist—John Muir
reporter—Barbara Walters
illustrator—Charles Schulz
congressperson—Shirley Chisholm

Is It Worth It?

Salary is frequently an important factor when considering a future career. But what other factors influence people to choose one career over another? Have students rank the following careers from one to ten (with one as the most important) on the basis of their value or importance to society: professional athlete, minister, actor, U.S. president, reporter, nurse, firefighter, teacher, banker, and astronaut. Compare and discuss the results in small groups. Which career(s) did the majority of students rank as most important? Least important? Emphasize that there are no right or wrong answers, but encourage each student to support his opinion.

Continue the discussion by pointing out that professional athletes and entertainers make much more money than teachers and ministers. Then have group members discuss the following questions, recording their opinions to share later with the class:

- Do the jobs deemed as most important to society pay the best salaries? Why do you think this is true?
- Should the jobs deemed as most important to society have high-paying salaries? Why or why not?
- What factors, besides salary, do you think attract people to these jobs?

Prominent Person Profile

Shirley Chisholm
Name Of Famous Person

Congresswoman
Name Of Career

Brittany Starr
Student

Shirley Chisholm was born in Brooklyn, New York, in 1924. She began her career as a nursery-school teacher. Later she became a day-care director in New York City. Shirley became the first black woman to serve in the United States Congress. She served from 1969–1983. In 1972 she campaigned for the Democratic presidential nomination, but she did not win. She is remembered for her commitment to help political parties and legislatures meet the needs of more citizens.

Career Interviews

The best information about careers comes from working people. Help students improve their oral skills while learning firsthand about careers by having them conduct interviews. Discuss the qualities of a good interview, using the guidelines below (which can be duplicated if desired). Many celebrities are interviewed on television. Consider showing the class a tape of a televised interview to help them see how the interviewer behaves. Duplicate "Planning A Career Interview" on page 33 for each student to use when planning his interview. Have each student plan a creative way to share his information with the class.

Interview Guidelines

1. Prepare and write out your interview questions ahead of time. Good interview questions require more than a *yes* or *no* answer. If the person being interviewed answers with *yes* or *no*, ask her to please explain her answer.

2. Decide on a time limit for your interview and stick to it. You'll be more likely to watch the clock, and the person being interviewed will appreciate you for honoring her busy schedule as well.

3. Come prepared with note paper, two pencils or pens, a working tape recorder, a recording tape, and your prepared list of questions.

4. Always ask the person being interviewed if she minds being recorded. Do not record if it makes the person uncomfortable.

5. The tape recorder is there to back you up. Take notes as you listen to answers, writing down good quotes or important words.

6. Don't let the person you're interviewing ramble. Gently and politely get her back on track with your prepared questions.

7. If a comment made by the person being interviewed leads you to ask a question that's not on your sheet, that's okay. Just be sure to get back to your line of questioning.

8. Be courteous. Remember that you represent your class and your school. Be sure to thank your interviewee before you leave the interview.

Patterns

Use with "Don't Forget Your Hat!" on page 26.

A Career Hat For: _____

Job Description: _____

Name: _____

©1996 The Education Center, Inc.

A Career Hat For: _____

Job Description: _____

Name: _____

©1996 The Education Center, Inc.

Name _____

Hats Off To A Lifetime Of Achievement!

You've just read about the lifetime career and achievements of a famous person. Share your facts and insights by completing of the following nine activities.

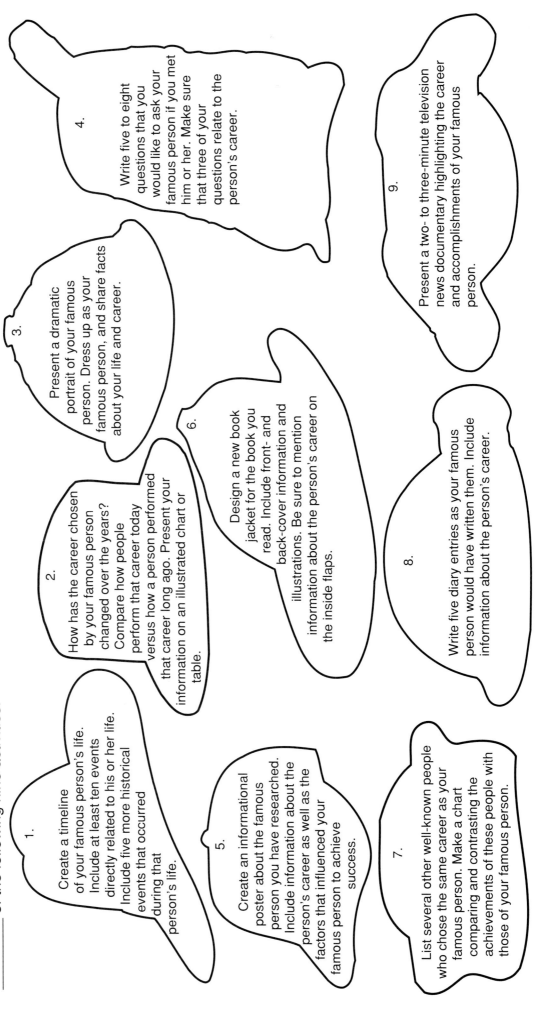

1.
Create a timeline of your famous person's life. Include at least ten events directly related to his or her life. Include five more historical events that occurred during that person's life.

2.
How has the career chosen by your famous person changed over the years? Compare how people perform that career today versus how a person performed that career long ago. Present your information on an illustrated chart or table.

3.
Present a dramatic portrait of your famous person. Dress up as your famous person, and share facts about your life and career.

4.
Write five to eight questions that you would like to ask your famous person if you met him or her. Make sure that three of your questions relate to the person's career.

5.
Create an informational poster about the famous person you have researched. Include information about the person's career as well as the factors that influenced your famous person to achieve success.

6.
Design a new book jacket for the book you read. Include front- and back-cover information and illustrations. Be sure to mention information about the person's career on the inside flaps.

7.
List several other well-known people who chose the same career as your famous person. Make a chart comparing and contrasting the achievements of these people with those of your famous person.

8.
Write five diary entries as your famous person would have written them. Include information about the person's career.

9.
Present a two- to three-minute television news documentary highlighting the career and accomplishments of your famous person.

Note To The Teacher: Use this reproducible with "We Tip Our Hats To You!" on page 27. Fill in the number of required activities above before duplicating this reproducible.

Pattern
Use with "Outstanding In Their Fields" on page 28.

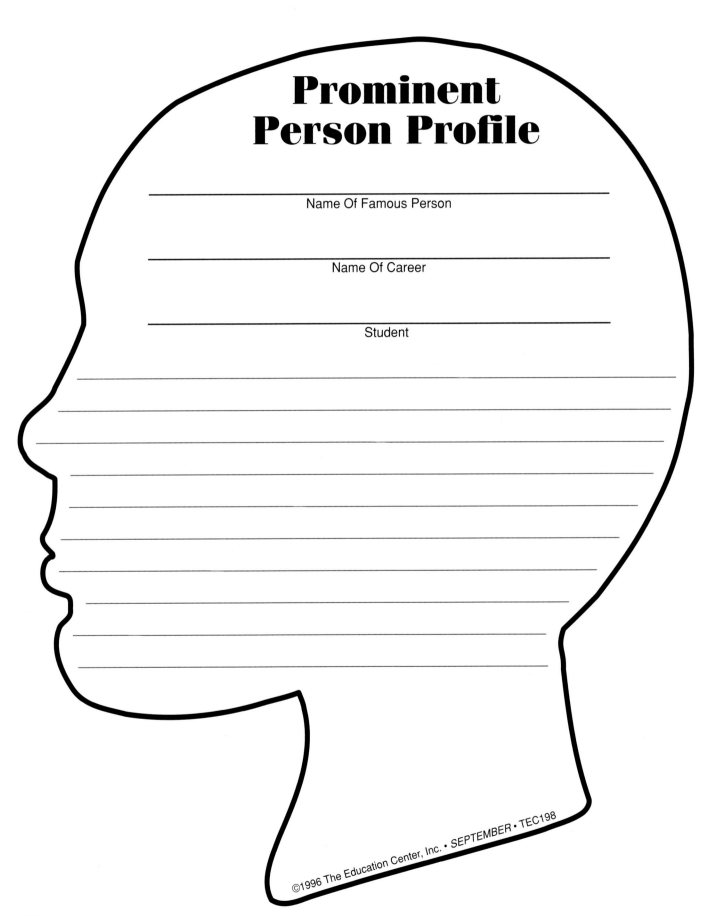

Prominent Person Profile

———————————————————
Name Of Famous Person

———————————————————
Name Of Career

———————————————————
Student

Planning A Career Interview

You can't pull a great interview out of a hat, but you can use this handy sheet to make your interview go smoothly. Fill out the information below to help you plan your interview.

Careers That Interest Me: _____

_____

Possible Interviewees: _____

_____

Confirmed Interviewee: _____

Date And Time Of Interview: _____

What I Want To Find Out: _____

_____

_____

_____

_____

My Interview Questions: _____

_____

_____

_____

_____

(Record actual interview notes on a separate sheet of paper stapled to this page.)

What I learned from my interview: _____

_____

_____

_____

_____

How I will share my research with the class: _____

_____

_____

Due Date: _____

Note To The Teacher: Use this reproducible with "Career Interviews" on page 29.

Tracking Down Self-Esteem

Activities To Help Students Develop Positive Self-Esteem

One thing all kids have in common is a need to feel good about themselves. Help build your students' self-esteem during the first month of school and all year long with the following fun activities!

Crack The Code!

What child doesn't enjoy figuring out a hidden message? And when the message is encouraging, it's even more fun! Challenge your students to put their heads together to design a class code using letters, numbers, or symbols. Provide each student with a copy of the final code to keep in his notebook. Each morning write an encouraging message—in code—on the board. Instruct students to decipher the message as soon as they've settled in for the day. Your code crackers will look forward to beginning each day on a positive—and mysteriously fun—note!

Daily Discoveries

Help students develop a sense of accomplishment and of moving forward by having them keep track of new things they learn each day. Create a poster like the one shown below, including a section for each subject you teach and an open area for any special events. Laminate the poster. At the end of each day, have one or more students use a wipe-off marker to write one thing they've learned on the poster. At the end of the week, have a student secretary copy all of the items into a notebook to review at the end of the year. Then wipe the poster clean for the next week.

A Symbol Of Me

Whether they realize it or not, students see symbols every day. Collect pictures of several easily recognizable symbols to share with your students: the McDonalds® golden arches, the Olympic rings, a dollar sign, the Nike® logo, etc. Discuss the meaning (or possible meaning) behind each symbol. Then challenge each student to design a symbol that represents her personality or accomplishments. Have her draw and color her symbol on a white paper plate. After each student has explained the meaning of her symbol, post the plates on a bulletin board titled "Look At Our Logos!"

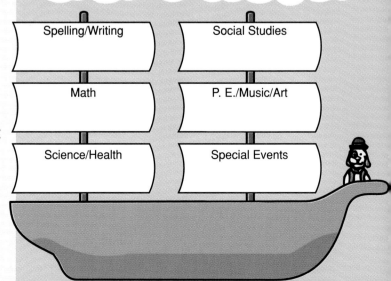

DAILY DISCOVERIES

Spelling/Writing	Social Studies
Math	P. E./Music/Art
Science/Health	Special Events

Boost Or Bust!

Help students realize that they have control over whether they feel good or bad about themselves. Instruct each child to list six *boosters*—actions or attitudes that will make her feel better about herself (getting plenty of exercise, practicing to become good in a sport, completing assignments on time, etc.). Then have her list six *busters*—actions or attitudes that cause her to feel negative about herself (watching too much television, missing a deadline for a project, comparing herself to others, etc.). Invite each student to share her boosters and busters with the class. Then give each child a 9" x 3" strip and a 1" x 2" strip of paper. Instruct the student to write a booster on the large strip and a buster on the small strip. Collect the small strips in a lunch-size paper bag.

Tell students that the bag represents the person who allows negative actions and attitudes to build. Blow up the bag; then ceremoniously pop it. Ask students, "Who gets hurt when negative actions and attitudes build up?" Of course, the person who has stored up the negativity suffers. However, the students' ears are also hurt by the loud noise that the bag makes. When we store up negative actions and attitudes, we often hurt others when we finally explode from the hurt. Finally arrange the booster strips on a wall as shown. Include the title "We're Taking The Right Steps!"

Tracking Down Emotions

Looking for ways to make students more aware of their emotions? Use the feeling words listed on the reproducible on page 44 as the basis for the following fun activities:

- Many of the words on the list will be new to your students. Use the list as vocabulary and spelling words.
- Duplicate the list; then cut apart the words and store them in a canister. Have the class sit in a circle. In turn have each student draw a word and tell about a time when he experienced that feeling.
- Duplicate a copy of page 44 for each student to keep in her notebook. During journal-writing time, encourage each student to choose one of the words and write about an event in her life that caused her to experience that feeling.
- Give each student a small paper bag. Have the student select one emotion from the list; then have him use crayons, markers, glue, and other art materials to transform his paper bag into a mask that displays that emotion. After the masks are made, have each student write a puppet skit that identifies a situation during which his emotion might be felt. (You may wish to pair up students for this activity.) After students have performed their puppet skits, mount the masks on a bulletin board with the caption "Masking Your Emotions."

Don't complain.

Do MY chores.

Hand in homework.

Get plenty of sleep.

Exercise.

Eat right!

POP

Now Featuring...

Overcome a student's shyness or hesitancy about sharing anything of a personal nature with this star-studded display. Enlarge the television announcer on page 42 to add to the board. Cut out four large stars (see the pattern on page 45) from yellow paper. Laminate the stars; then add them to the display as shown. Duplicate a class list. Cut the names apart and store them in an envelope. Each week hold a drawing to pick the student of the week. Use a wipe-off marker to label the top star with the honored child's name. Then use the activities that follow on this page and on pages 37 and 38 to add a variety of self-esteem-building components to the display.

★ Personal Preferences ★

Want to know what tickles your students' fancy? At the beginning of the year, give students the reproducible on page 46. Students will complete the open-ended statements and then support them with reasons. File the forms. Each week mount the student of the week's completed form on one of the star shapes on the bulletin board.

★ Your Life And Times ★

Here's a different way to have students share autobiographical information. Give each student a copy of the reproducible on page 47. On the form, the student will highlight important events in his life using a timeline format, then fill in information about family members, places he has lived or visited, special hobbies he enjoys, etc. Display the student of the week's sheet on one of the board's star cutouts.

★ A Personal Silhouette ★

Enlist the assistance of a parent volunteer to help you make a silhouette of each student. To create a silhouette, tape an 18" x 24" sheet of black paper to a wall. Position a chair on the floor in front of the paper so that when the student sits down and a light is directed her way, a profile of the student's head can be traced. Cut out each outline; then store the silhouettes for later use. Mount the student of the week's silhouette on one of the star cutouts.

★ A Booklet Of Compliments ★

Challenge students to give compliments instead of cuts! Give all students except the one being spotlighted a star-shaped cutout (see the pattern on page 45) or a Post-It® Brand note. Ask students to think of a one-sentence compliment about the student of the week. Circulate a sheet of lined paper. Have each student record his compliment on this sheet, making sure it is different from those already on the list; then have him write his compliment on the star cutout or Post-It® note. Staple the compliments around the three larger stars on the board. When it is time to spotlight the next student, staple these compliments together to make a minibooklet. Give the booklet to the student of the week to take home.

Susan has a very happy smile!

Susan is always helpful in our group.

37

★ A Personal Diamante ★

A *diamante* is a form of poetry that has seven lines and takes the shape of a diamond (see the diagram and example). Have each child write several diamantes about herself and select her favorite one. Provide the student with a copy of the diamond-shaped form on page 45. After the student copies her poem on the form, have her cut it out and glue it onto a sheet of colored paper. Direct the student to trim the colored paper, leaving a one-inch border around the poem. Add the student of the week's diamante to the display on page 36; or post the diamantes on a bulletin board titled "Personal Poetry."

Line 1: First name
Line 2: Two adjectives that describe your feelings about school
Line 3: Three verbs telling what you like to do
Line 4: A phrase that connects the other lines (write this one last)
Line 5: Three verbs telling what you are good at doing
Line 6: Two adjectives that describe how you feel about yourself
Line 7: Last name

Brent
serious, successful
listens to music, bicycles, skateboards
a fifth-grade student at Lakeland Elementary School
plays baseball, draws cars, makes milkshakes
content, happy
Thompson

★ Star Talents ★

Invite your class to go stargazing with this activity! Help students understand the difference between a *talent* (a natural or learned ability to do something) and an *accomplishment* (using that ability to execute and successfully complete an action). Suggest examples of talented people; then have students brainstorm a list of talents and discuss how these talents can be used to accomplish certain feats. For example, if a person is well coordinated *(a talent)*, he may be able to play baseball or swim on a team *(an accomplishment)*. Give each student a copy of the reproducible on page 48 that has been duplicated on yellow paper. Ask him to write his talents and accomplishments on the star. Then have students cut out their stars and share them with the class. Save these stars to use later for the bulletin board on page 36.

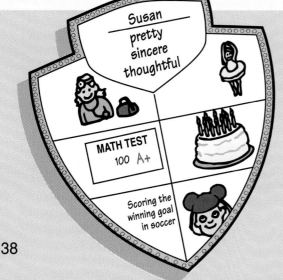

★ A Personal Shield ★

Shield your students against doubts of self-worth by having them make pieces of armor to combat negative thoughts. Duplicate the shield pattern on page 49 for each student. Direct students to list words, or draw a picture or symbol, for each of the shield's numbered spaces as described on the pattern page. Add a child's shield to the display during his special week.

A Rose By Any Other Name...

Students can be very creative in ridiculing their classmates. One favorite target is a person's name. Survey students to find out how many have had others make fun of their names. Then read *Chrysanthemum* by Kevin Henkes (published by Greenwillow Books). This humorous picture book describes how a little mouse named Chrysanthemum deals with her classmates' ridicule of her name. Use the story to generate discussion about peer mocking and how to handle it. Ask students, "How did Chrysanthemum's classmates make her feel? What realizations made Chrysanthemum feel better about her name?" Discuss the positive steps and attitudes students can adopt to help them cope with peer ridicule.

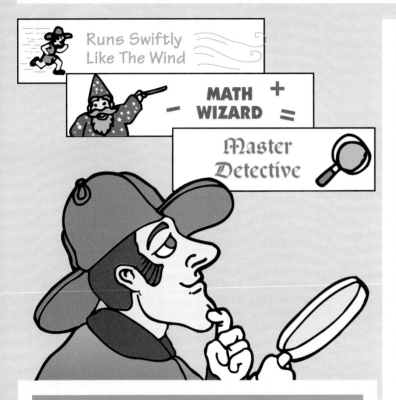

Making A Name For Myself

Your name—it's the label you respond to, but does it say anything about who you are as a person? Give each student a chance to create a new name for himself. Have each child reflect on one thing in his life that makes him unique; then have him create a name for himself that illustrates that special quality. For example, a student who loves to run fast may name himself "Runs Swiftly Like The Wind." Ask each child to share his name and its meaning with the rest of the class.

Next give each student a tagboard strip on which to write his new name and add illustrations. Have the student place two small pieces of magnetic tape on the back of the strip at the ends; then have him mount the strip on his desk for a handy desktag of distinction!

Wanted: A Good Friend!

Nothing makes someone feel better than to have a good friend. Encourage students to think about what it takes to be a friend by creating a class poster about friendship. Begin by having each student make two lists: "What A Good Friend Will Do" and "What A Good Friend Will Not Do." Have students take turns sharing their lists while you write the characteristics named most often on the board. After the sharing time, have a student draw a friendly face at the top of a piece of poster board. Under the picture, make two columns listing the most popular characteristics named by students. Display the poster as a reminder of what it means to be a friend. *Adapted from an idea by Dorsay Howard, Johnson Street Elementary School, High Point, NC*

WANTED:
A Good Friend!

A good friend will...	A good friend will not...
greet you with a smile. help you when you need help. remember your birthday.	hold a grudge. leave you when you need him or her. make fun of you.

The White-Hat Squad

Envision posses of students searching for "good guys" in your classroom, and you've got an idea of how "The White-Hat Squad" can promote self-esteem. Explain to students that early westerns tended to depict the good guys wearing white cowboy hats. Announce that you will give a White-Hat Award each week to a "good-guy" student who tries to help others feel good about themselves. Allow students to nominate classmates by writing a description of a kind deed they've observed and submitting it to you. (Make sure nominating students also include their names on the nominations.) At the end of each week, select a winning student. Recognize the winner and the classmate who nominated her by photographing the two together, each wearing a white cowboy hat or baseball cap. Display the photo in a prominent place for all to see.

Fleeting Emotions

Explore a variety of emotions and release pent-up energy with this "emotional" race. To prepare, cut a supply of paper strips. Write an emotion on each strip (see page 44 for a list of emotions). Divide the class into equal teams. Have each team select a dealer, who stands at the goal line. Line up each team at the finish line (about 10 to 15 feet from the goal line). Give each dealer one strip. On your command, have one student from each team run to the goal line, take the strip of paper from his dealer, and act out the emotion—using only sounds and gestures. If his team does not correctly guess the emotion after three tries, the member must race back to the finish line and tag the next teammate. That player runs to the goal line and gets a new emotion to act out from her dealer. Award teams one point for each correct answer.

It's My Bag

Play this guessing game with students to see how well they really know their classmates. Ask each student to bring five items from home—stored in a paper grocery bag—that represent her personal attributes or interests. Collect the bags; then divide the class into teams. Empty one bag at a time onto a table in front of the class. Allow team members to discuss the bag's contents and to reach a consensus about the owner's identity. After all teams have made a guess as to the bag's owner, have the owner identify himself. Award one point for each correct guess. At the end of the game, evaluate the reasons why each group guessed the way it did. Also let students share reasons for their choices of items.

The Do's And Don'ts Of Friendship

Capitalize on the wealth of opportunities for teaching friendship skills offered by Eleanor Estes's book, *The Hundred Dresses* (Harcourt Brace Jovanovich, Publishers). Read this short book aloud to your class or have it read in small groups. Ask students to respond (either in writing or verbally) to the following themes from the book. Then have them offer solutions or coping strategies for similar real-life situations.

- Peer pressure *(Refer to Maddie's not taking up for Wanda and her fear of becoming the next target of teasing.)*
- Guilt *(Refer to Maddie's personal feelings about being involved with the dresses game.)*
- Forgiveness *(Refer to the realization, too late, that the dresses game was a mistake or to the reason Wanda had for making the drawings of the dresses.)*
- Unkind words *(Refer to the examples of teasing.)*
- Loneliness *(Elicit from students specific clues that point to Wanda's loneliness.)*
- Truthfulness *(Ask students why they think Wanda lied about the dresses.)*
- Judging others *(Relate this to Wanda's outward appearance and her inner self-worth.)*

Acting Up!

Help students recognize the importance of body language as a communication tool by playing Emotional Charades. Before the game, write short descriptions of emotional situations on separate slips of paper (see the suggestions below). Divide the class into groups of two or three students each. Give each group one situation to practice. Instruct students that they may use gestures and sounds—but no words—to portray their situations. When the groups have prepared, have each act out its situation. Challenge the other groups to guess what's going on and what emotions the characters in each skit may be feeling. Discuss how body language helped students identify a situation or how a character was feeling.

Sample situations:
A mother hurrying her child(ren) off to school
Two students approaching the principal's office after getting in trouble
Children waiting to surprise a friend at his birthday party
A child cheering up a sad friend
Two friends getting on a roller coaster
A child who finds his little brother messing with his personal belongings
Two students who have had an argument, but then talk it out and make up

41

Needless Worries?

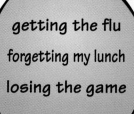

Many of the things students worry about never happen, and if they do, they're usually not as bad as anticipated. Lead a discussion about the kinds of things students worry about: being disliked or left out, making bad grades, having parents divorce, getting sick, etc. Make two columns on the board: "What I Worry About And Can Control" and "What I Worry About And Can't Control." Have groups brainstorm situations that could be listed under each category. Then let them suggest ways to resolve the situations they *can* control. For example, if a student is worried about an upcoming test, she can turn off the TV and study.

Next have students brainstorm things they could do to help themselves worry less about situations they *can't* control. For example, instead of worrying about Dad's upcoming plane trip, the student can channel his energy into making a welcome-home banner. Help students see that every attempt they make toward resolving a situation decreases the amount of anxiety they feel.

Finally challenge each child to keep a private diary for one week. In the diary, the child should list all the things she worries about during that week. At the end of the week, have students determine how many of their worries actually came to pass. For a ceremonious conclusion to this activity, give each student a balloon and a felt-tipped marker. Have her blow up the balloon, knot it, and then write each worry that didn't materialize on the balloon. Allow her to pop the balloon and banish those worries forever!

Pattern

Use with "Now Featuring..." on page 36.

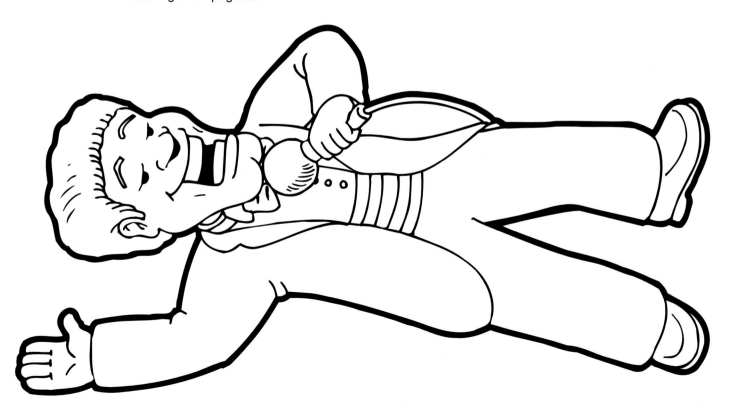

My Thought For The Day

Help your students learn more about themselves by reflecting on one of the following incomplete thoughts each day of the month. Use these thoughts to start a class discussion or generate journal writing. If desired, duplicate a copy of the grid for each student to keep in her notebook.

Something that makes me laugh is…	The thing I'm most concerned about is…	My favorite time of the day is _____ because…	If I could take lessons to learn about something new, I would want to learn…	Something I'm really good at is…
Wishes can become goals for life. If I had three wishes, they would be…	If I went on a trip and could take only one possession, I would take…	I get angry when…	If I could make an outstanding contribution to the world, I would…	There are times when I like to be alone. One of these times is when…
There are times when I like to be with others. One of these times is…	When I grow up, I want to make a living by…	I can't _____ but I can… I won't _____ but I will… I don't _____ but I do…	If I could plan my perfect vacation, it would be…	On the timeline of my life, the event that stands out the most is…
I feel important when…	If I were president, the first thing I would do is…	The first thing that I'd like a stranger to know about me is…	I seem to get my way when…	I like to hear stories about…

Tracking Down Emotions

abandoned	delighted	impressed	relieved
affectionate	depressed	infatuated	restless
agonized	destructive	inspired	sad
alone	determined	interested	satisfied
ambivalent	different	intimidated	scared
angry	distracted	jealous	secure
annoyed	disturbed	joyful	sensitive
anxious	dominated	kind	silly
apathetic	eager	lazy	sneaky
awed	earnest	lonely	sorrowful
bad	empty	lost	spiteful
betrayed	energetic	loving	stupid
bitter	envious	low	sulky
bold	evil	lucky	suspicious
bored	excited	mad	sympathetic
brave	exhausted	mean	talkative
calm	fearful	miserable	tempted
capable	foolish	nervous	tense
challenged	frantic	nutty	terrible
cheated	free	obnoxious	terrified
cheerful	frightened	obsessed	threatened
childish	frustrated	odd	tired
clever	glad	outraged	trapped
combative	good	overwhelmed	troubled
competitive	greedy	panicked	ugly
concerned	grief-stricken	pathetic	uncertain
confident	guilty	peaceful	uneasy
confused	happy	persecuted	unhappy
contented	hateful	pity	unsure
courageous	helpful	pleased	useless
cruel	helpless	pressured	violent
crushed	homesick	pretty	weepy
curious	honored	proud	wicked
deceitful	horrible	quarrelsome	wonderful
defeated	hurt	rejected	worrisome
dejected	ignored	relaxed	zany

Note To The Teacher: Use this page with "Tracking Down Emotions" on page 35 and "Fleeting Emotions" on page 40.

Use with "A Personal Diamante" on page 38.

Name _____ *Interest inventory*

A Few Of My Favorite Things

Favorite people, favorite places, favorite things—everyone has favorites!
Fill in the blanks below and share what makes your best-liked list!

1. My favorite TV program is _____ because _____
   _____ .

2. My favorite book is _____ because _____
   _____ .

3. My favorite song is _____ because _____
   _____ .

4. My favorite movie is _____ because _____
   _____ .

5. My favorite color is _____ because _____
   _____ .

6. My favorite animal is the _____ because _____
   _____ .

7. My favorite sport is _____ because _____
   _____ .

8. My favorite hobby is _____ because _____
   _____ .

9. My favorite thing to wear is _____ because _____
   _____ .

10. My favorite game to play with a friend is _____ because _____
    _____ .

11. My favorite saying is _____ because _____
    _____ .

12. My favorite actor is _____ because _____
    _____ .

13. My favorite actress is _____ because _____
    _____ .

14. My favorite holiday is _____ because _____
    _____ .

15. My favorite TV commercial is _____ because _____
    _____ .

When you're finished, color the border with your favorite colors!

©1996 The Education Center, Inc. • *SEPTEMBER* • TEC198

Note To The Teacher: Use with "Personal Preferences" on page 36.

★ ★

The Life And Times Of

★ ★

Vol. 10   Date: 50¢

My Family

_____
_____
_____
_____
_____
_____
_____
_____
_____
_____

I'll Never Forget...

_____
_____
_____
_____
_____
_____
_____
_____
_____
_____
_____
_____

Places I've Visited

_____
_____
_____
_____
_____
_____
_____
_____

A Special Interest

_____
_____
_____
_____
_____

★ ★ ★ ★ ★ ★ ★ ★ ★ ★ ★ ★ ★ ★ ★ ★ ★ ★ ★ ★

Important Dates In My Life
(in order, starting with the earliest event)

Date: _____   Event: _____

Date: _____   Event: _____

Date: _____   Event: _____

Date: _____   Event: _____

★ ★ ★ ★ ★ ★ ★ ★ ★ ★ ★ ★ ★ ★ ★ ★ ★ ★ ★ ★

Note To The Teacher: Use with "Your Life And Times" on page 37.

Star Talents

You—yes, *you*—are a talented individual! Everyone has talents. And if you use your talents, you can accomplish incredible things! Take some time to think about your talents. Write each talent on a blank in the star. In the star point above each talent, write something you've accomplished because you have that ability. When you're finished, decorate the middle of your star with your name. Use your creative talents (you've got them, too!) to make your name really eye-catching.

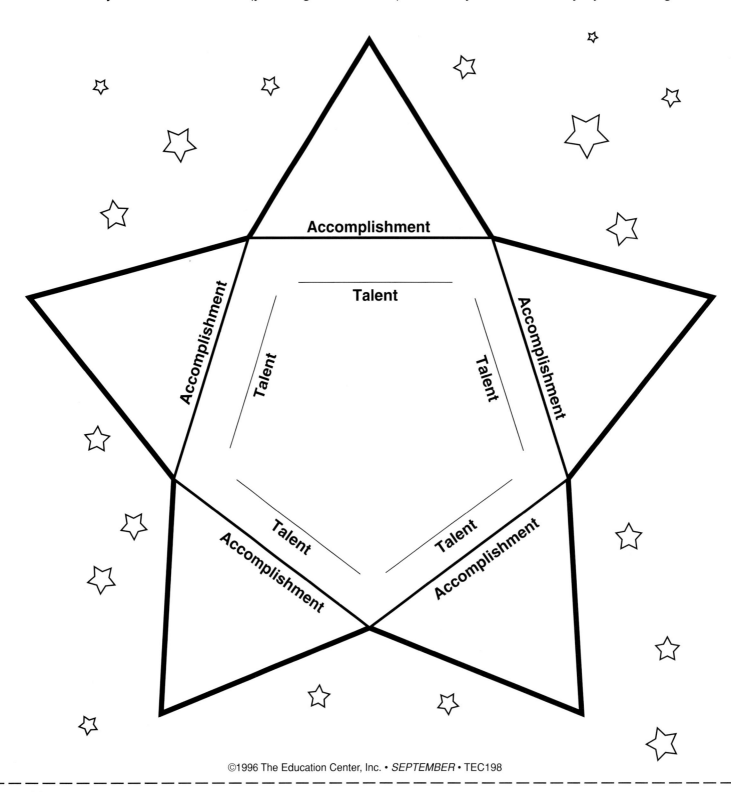

Note To The Teacher: Use with "Star Talents" on page 38.

Protection Against Negative Thoughts

Sometimes life can be hard, and you might need a little armor to protect you against feeling bad about yourself. Take a look at the shield below. For each section, list words or draw a picture or symbol according to the key.

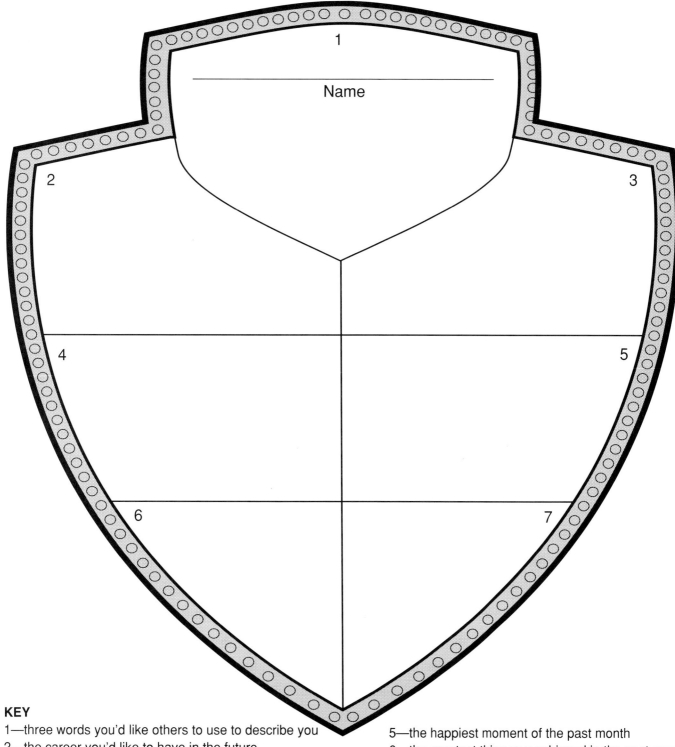

KEY

1—three words you'd like others to use to describe you
2—the career you'd like to have in the future
3—something you do well
4—something you were successful at this week

5—the happiest moment of the past month
6—the greatest thing you achieved in the past year
7—the most memorable, happiest event of your life

Note To The Teacher: Use with "A Personal Shield" on page 38.

Taking Open House To New Heights

Follow these blueprints for your most successful Open House yet!

Pop-Up Invitations

Grab parents' attention with both the wording and the design of a pop-up-style invitation. Provide students with 9" x 11" sheets of white construction paper. Instruct them to fold and cut the paper according to the reproducible directions on page 55. Have students copy the specific information you want included on the invitation from the board. Supply colored pencils to use for coloring. Send the invitations home.

WANTED: Your Attendance At Open House!

When: Sept. 9th at 7:30

Where: Greenfield Elementary

- Watch your child star in a video!
- Take a trip around the classroom!
- Participate in activities with your child!
- Ask questions, get answers!
- Meet teachers, parents!
- Win door prizes!

We Want To See You There!

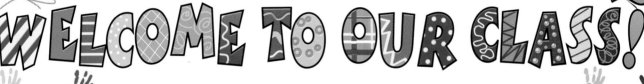

WELCOME TO OUR CLASS!

Josh Callie Johnny Rico Peter Sarah Tad

Jenny Cathy Allie Michael Grant Allen Rich

Handprinted Welcome Banner

Personalize your classroom's welcome banner by having students make and decorate it. Provide markers to color in the letters of a handmade or computer-generated banner. Set out aluminum pie pans that contain fall-colored paint. Have students give the banner individual stamps of approval by making fall-colored handprints around the wording. Be sure to have the students autograph their imprints after the imprints have dried.

Courtney is a friend to all.

The Apples Of My Eye

Teachers are the usual recipients of apples, right? Give this custom an unexpected twist by providing apples for the parents! Prior to Open House, cut a paper leaf for each child; then write a complimentary statement on it. After laminating the leaves, tape each leaf to the stem of an apple. Place the apples on the children's desks. Parents will enjoy reading comments like "Adam is the apple of my eye because he always leaves his desk in order," or "Courtney is a friend to all."

Around The Room In 20 Minutes

Invite parents on a whirlwind classroom tour! Ahead of time, tape laminated paper arrows to the floor to show the path to follow. Duplicate a list of the stops along the tour. *(Possible tour stops include: parent sign-in sheet as the first stop; science, social studies, or art displays; bulletin boards; various centers; classroom rules-and-consequences chart; student-of-the-week board; announcements board; homework board; and birthday calendar.)* At each stop display a sign that gives a brief explanation of the activity at that site. Post a student at the *Start* arrow to hand out lists. Also assign students to each tour stop to answer parents' questions.

Door Prizes Do The Trick!

Offering freebies as bait is a successful way to lure parents to Open House—and they don't have to be expensive ones, either! Tie an inflated balloon to each door prize: a school pencil, an inexpensive houseplant, a small notepad, a paperback book, a Tootsie Roll® lollipop, a canned soft drink, a wrapped brownie or cookie, a pack of LifeSavers®, or a candy bar. Imagine how uplifted parents will feel when they enter your room and are then struck with the sight of different-colored balloons!

A Walk Down Memory Lane

Dust the cobwebs from parents' memories by inviting them to reminisce about their days in grade school. A week or so prior to the scheduled Open House, send home the reproducible on page 56. Request that parents prick their memories and write about the kind of school they attended, how they got to school, what they did after school, the kind of lunches served in their cafeteria, what their favorite school lunch was, who their best friend was, what their favorite recess game was, etc. Ask that they complete the form and return it to school—submitting as many memories as they'd like. Post all responses on a bulletin board titled "Walking With Parents Down Memory Lane."

> **Lunchtime**
> I remember I always took my lunch on Fridays because the cafeteria would serve soup that day made from the week's leftovers...
>
> Kimberley Jones — Child
> John Jones — Parent

Rising Stars

Bring out the ham in students and surely increase parents' attendance at Open House with this impromptu-styled activity. Videotape each student completing the following statement(s):

- "What I like best about school is…."
- "If I were principal for a day, I would…."
- "Someday I would like to be a…because…."

At Open House simply start the video, relax, and let the kids shine!

"Guess Who?" Hanging Mobiles

Have some fun by challenging parents to find their own child's desk. Earlier in the week have each student make his own three-paneled mobile. Give each student three sheets of 8 1/2" x 11" white paper. Ask the student to attach a silhouette or baby picture of himself to one sheet and then make his handprints (using paint) on the second sheet. Instruct the student to write a four- to five-line riddle about himself on a third sheet. Have each white sheet stapled to a 9" x 12" sheet of colored paper. Then have a long edge of one panel stapled to a long edge of the second panel. Continue until all three panels have been stapled side-to-side in a triangular shape. Punch one hole at the top of each colored sheet; then tie a length of yarn through each of the holes. Join the yarn lengths and attach them to a jumbo-sized, bent paper clip. Suspend each student's three-dimensional mobile over his desk. At Open House ask each parent to walk around the room, study the clues she finds on the mobiles, and sit at her child's desk when she has identified it.

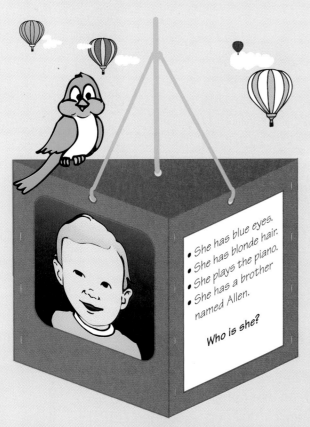

- She has blue eyes.
- She has blonde hair.
- She plays the piano.
- She has a brother named Allen.

Who is she?

"Purr-sonal" Puzzles

Find out how well parents *really* know their children when you ask them to work these puzzles! Provide each student with an enlarged copy of one of the reproducibles from page 57 or page 58. When the puzzle forms have been completed, laminate them and then return them to the students. Ask each student to cut the pieces apart, place them inside an envelope, and write "_____'s 'Purr-sonal' Puzzle" on the outside of the envelope. Also have students use an inkpad to stamp several of their thumbprints on the envelopes. Then provide markers and allow the students to create cats and other animals from their thumbprints.

At Open House have fun observing the looks on parents' faces as they work to assemble the puzzles AND learn more about their child at the same time. Allow parents to take the keepsake home with them.

Peter's "Purr-sonal" Puzzle

Sign-Up Sheets

Don't allow those important parent sign-up sheets to go unnoticed. Alert parents to their locations by creating attention-grabbing signs that can't be missed due to their unexpected sizes or shapes. Use creative symbols, wild colors, or clever phrasing. For example, design a sign in the shape of a large, colorful, and decorative party hat on which you've boldly written the words "Let's Party!" Place a similarly designed sign-up sheet for classroom parties on a table or desk near the sign (see the example). Or tape a sign-up sheet to each student's desk—taping it ensures that parents won't accidentally take it home! Use this method for obtaining grade parents to help supervise on field trips, serve as classroom volunteers, or perform clerical work.

"Let's Party!" Sign-Up Sheet

Christmas

Name   I'll Provide   I'll Be There To Help

Valentine's Day

Name   I'll Provide   I'll Be There To Help

End-Of-The-Year

Name   I'll Provide   I'll Be There To Help

Open House Jeopardy®

Try using this game-show format to introduce parents to daily schedules, curriculum areas, and other important information. Use a marker to make a blank 6 x 5 grid on an overhead transparency. Fill in categories and answers on the grid similar to the format on the Jeopardy® game show. Designate categories like Mark The Spot, It's Time, Who's Who, etc. Include answers like "This person helps us warm up our muscles before we exercise or play a game," "We do this every day from 12:00 to 12:30," or "This is where the week's lunch menu is posted." Cover the answers with Post-it® Brand notes labeled with point values instead of cash amounts.

Team up parents with their children (parents will probably need their children's help!), and then divide the group into two teams. Have a parent on Team One select a category and a point value. Have her respond in question form—just like on the television version. If she answers correctly, award Team One that number of points and allow another turn. If answered incorrectly, allow a parent on Team Two to respond to the same answer. If he answers correctly, award Team Two the points and allow him to make the next selection. Continue play until the grid has been entirely uncovered. Declare the team with the highest point total the winners. Then reward the winners with inexpensive door prizes or other treats.

Open House Tote Bags

Not enough hands to hold all those Open House handouts? Here's a handy solution to ensure that they will make it home with parents. Save paper grocery sacks. Have each student cut a handle for his parent's bag from a scrap of laminated paper and staple it in place. Provide paints, brushes, markers, and other materials; then allow the students to create "signature bags" for their parents to use at Open House.

No-Mistake-About-It Nametags

End forever those embarrassing introductions sometimes encountered when a remarried parent has a different last name from his child. Use nametags that include lines for both the child's name and the parent's name (see the handy patterns on page 55). Then, when meeting the parent for the first time, you've reduced the chance of getting off on the wrong foot.

Not The Usual Form

Capitalize on the Open House format to gather helpful information that can be used later during parent conferences or throughout the year. Duplicate copies of the reproducible on page 59 and place it on each student's desk for Open House. Ask that the parent sit down and answer (with the child's help) questions on this very different form—questions like "What are your child's strongest academic subjects?" and "What should be your child's three main academic goals for the first nine weeks?" You'll receive data that identifies a student's learning style from questions like "When your child receives a gift that needs to be assembled, does he read the directions first, or does he dive right in and try to figure it out as he goes?" Use the information gained to help you focus on individual student needs, to make lesson plans, and to conduct conferences.

Team Spirit

Capture the rampant spirit of teamwork at Open House with an instant picture! Ahead of time prepare a bulletin board titled "We Make A Strong Team." Also make simple, paper miniframes for the photos you will take by slightly folding inward the four sides of five-inch squares of paper. Staple the miniframes to the board so that the photos can be added right after they're taken. Enlist a volunteer for Open House (hubbies or beaus are great at this!) to snap a photo of you posing between each parent and his child. When the bulletin board is taken down, send the framed photos home to the parents as keepsakes.

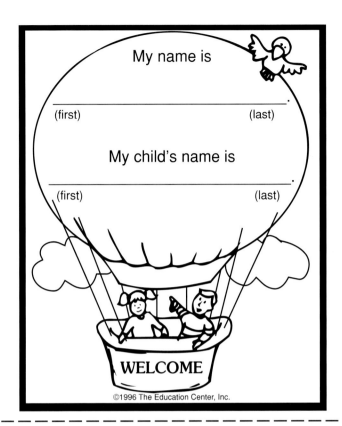

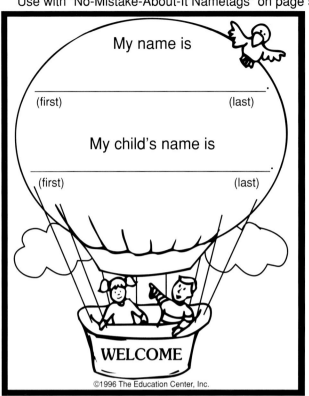

Name _____   *Open House: invitation*

You're Invited!

Get ready for Open House by making this high-flyin', fun invitation!

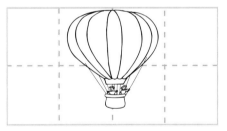

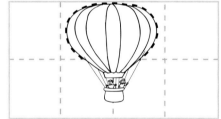

1. Fold your paper into eight sections; then unfold the paper.

2. Draw a hot-air balloon shape so that it extends above the horizontal fold as shown.

3. Using sharp scissors or an art knife, cut along the dark dotted line as shown.

4. Fold the top half of the paper back along the horizontal fold. Pull up the cut-out portion as shown.

5. Copy the information about your Open House from the chalkboard onto the invitation. Color the invitation.

©1996 The Education Center, Inc. • *SEPTEMBER* • TEC198

Note To The Teacher: Use with "Pop-Up Invitations" on page 50. Provide each student with a copy of these directions, a sheet of white construction paper, sharp scissors or an art knife (used with supervision), and markers or crayons.

55

Open House: bulletin-board project

A Walk Down Memory Lane

Ask your parents to complete the following assignment: Have them reminisce with you about what school was like for them when they were in the same grade that you are in now. Prick their memories about the kinds of schools they attended, how they got to school, what they did after school, the kinds of lunches their cafeterias served, what their favorite school lunches were, who their best friends were, what their favorite recess games were, etc. Ask them to write about their school memories in the form below—recollecting as many memories as they'd like. Cut out the form along its border and return it to school.

(title)

Child: _____

Parent: _____

Note To The Teacher: Use with "A Walk Down Memory Lane" on page 51.

Pattern

Use with " 'Purr-sonal' Puzzles" on page 52. See pattern for girls on page 58.

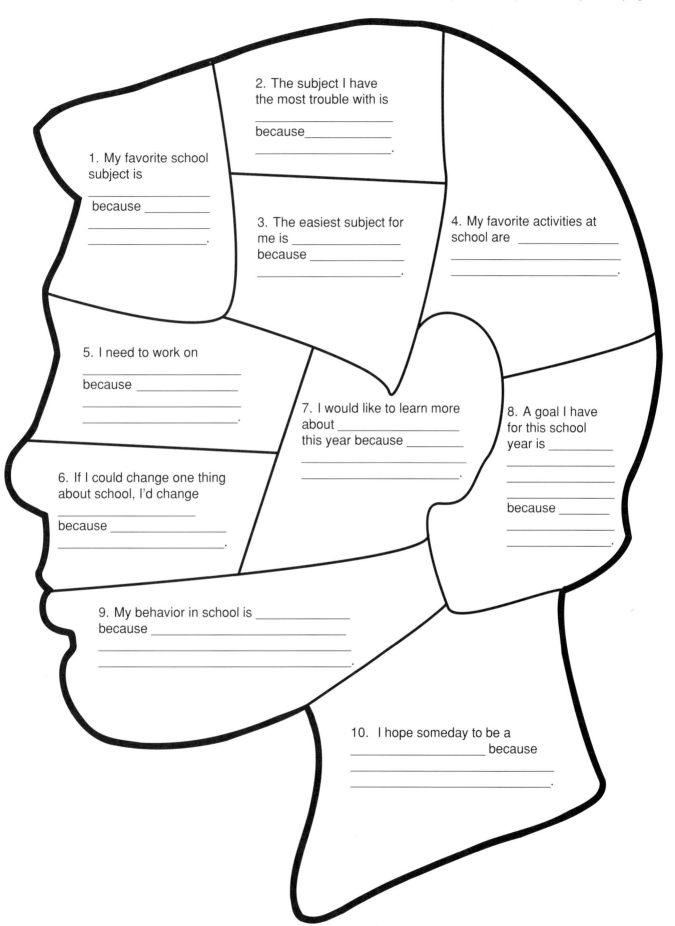

1. My favorite school subject is

because _____
_____
_____.

2. The subject I have the most trouble with is

_____
because_____
_____.

3. The easiest subject for me is _____
because _____
_____.

4. My favorite activities at school are _____

_____
_____.

5. I need to work on

because _____
_____
_____.

6. If I could change one thing about school, I'd change
_____
because _____
_____.

7. I would like to learn more about _____
this year because _____

_____
_____.

8. A goal I have for this school year is _____
_____
_____
_____

because _____
_____
_____.

9. My behavior in school is _____
because _____
_____
_____.

10. I hope someday to be a
_____ because
_____
_____.

Pattern

Use with " 'Purr-sonal' Puzzles" on page 52. See pattern for boys on page 57.

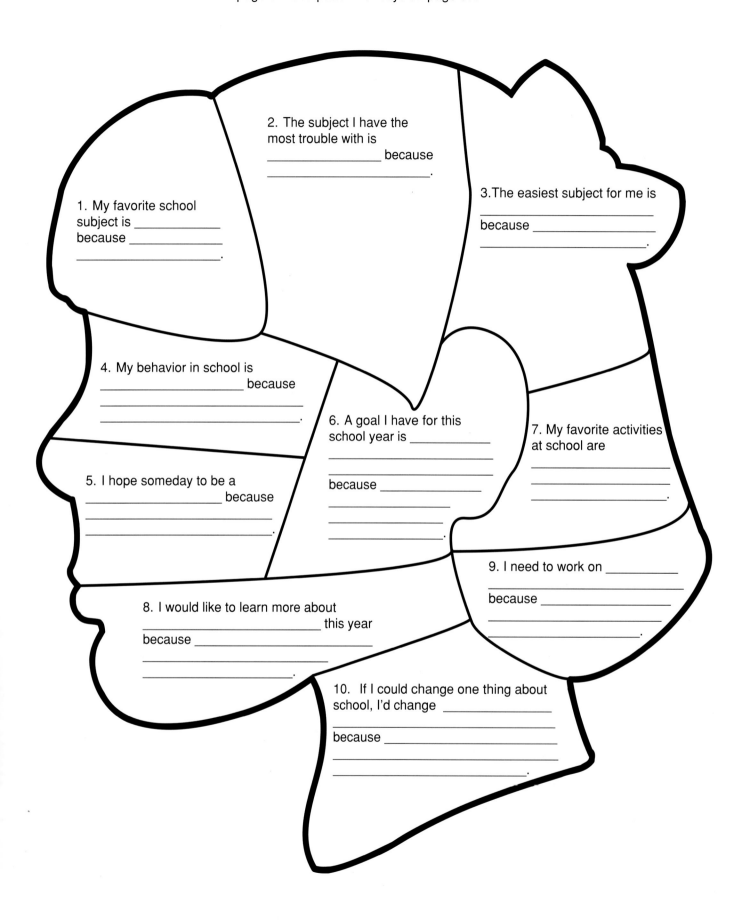

1. My favorite school subject is _____ because _____ _____.

2. The subject I have the most trouble with is _____ because _____.

3. The easiest subject for me is _____ because _____ _____.

4. My behavior in school is _____ because _____ _____.

5. I hope someday to be a _____ because _____ _____.

6. A goal I have for this school year is _____ _____ because _____ _____ _____.

7. My favorite activities at school are _____ _____ _____.

8. I would like to learn more about _____ this year because _____ _____ _____.

9. I need to work on _____ because _____ _____ _____.

10. If I could change one thing about school, I'd change _____ because _____ _____ _____.

Name _____

 # Parent-Child Questionnaire

Please take a moment to answer each of the following questions as carefully and thoughtfully as you can. Then return the form to your child's teacher. Use the back if you need more space.

1. What are your child's major interests? _____
_____

2. What are your child's strongest academic subjects? _____
_____

3. What are your child's weakest academic subjects? _____
_____

4. Which reading skill(s) would you like to see strengthened? _____
_____

5. Which math skill(s) would you like to see strengthened? _____
_____

6. Which writing skill(s) would you like to see strengthened? _____
_____

7. Which study skill(s) would you like to see strengthened? _____
_____

8. What should be your child's three main academic goals for the first nine weeks? _____
_____

9. When your child receives a gift that needs to be assembled, does he read the directions first, or does he dive right in and try to figure it out as he goes? _____

10. Is your child more apt to complete a three-step direction if you simply give him oral instructions, or do you need to write the instructions for your child? _____
_____

11. Would your child rather watch television or play outside? _____

12. Does your child prefer listening to music or reading a book? _____

13. If your child could choose the subjects he studied in school, what would he choose? _____
_____

14. Which would your child prefer to do: write a story, read a story, or act out a story? _____

15. Would your child rather make a craft after hearing the directions, reading the directions, or watching someone make a sample? _____

16. Do you read to your child? _____   If so, how often? _____

17. If you do read to your child, is it done on a school night, during the weekend, or both? _____
_____

Note To The Teacher: Use with "Not The Usual Form" on page 54.

We The People

Activities For Teaching About The Constitution And U.S. Government

"We the people"—these three small words begin an important document that touches the lives of your students every day. Use the following activities to introduce your young citizens to our country's government during Constitution Week (September 17–23) or any time of the year.

Why Do We Need The Constitution?

"Why do we have to study this?" Help students make the connection between the Constitution and their own lives by asking a simple question: "What would life be like if there were no rules?" To help students visualize such a concept, ask them, "What would a baseball game without rules be like? A busy intersection in New York City? A family with six children?" Lead the class in a discussion about the results of living without rules; then ask students to explain the purpose behind rules *(rules tell us what to do).* Explain that the U.S. Constitution basically tells Americans what to do and how our government (our system of rules) will be run.

The Honorable Ann Mize
United States Senate
Washington, DC 20510

Dear Senator

Invite your state's top politicians to join your Constitution Week activities. Help the class compose a simple letter asking your state or congressional senators to answer these questions:

- Why is the Constitution important to our country?
- What do you think is the most important thing about being a U.S. citizen?
- Why did you decide to work in our government?
- What advice would you have for students who want to get involved in government?

Increase your chances of receiving a prompt reply by enclosing a self-addressed, stamped envelope with each letter. Or enclose a blank cassette tape for a taped reply. (For an address to use when writing a U.S. senator, see page 66.)

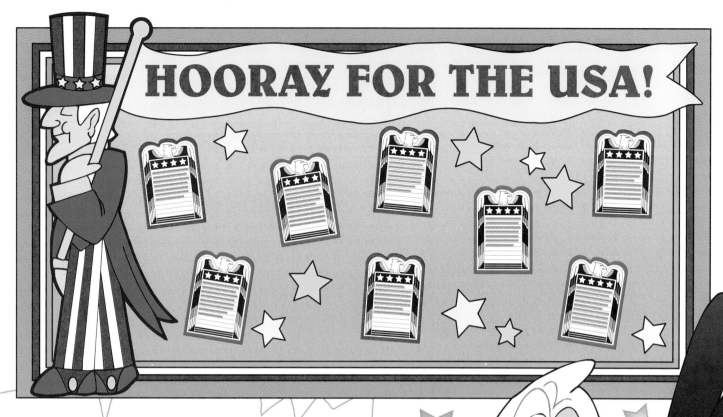

HOORAY FOR THE USA!

"I Pledge…"

Students may not realize that saying the pledge to the flag means that the speaker is promising to be loyal to the Constitution and laws of the United States. In Bette Bao Lord's excellent children's novel, *In The Year Of The Boar And Jackie Robinson*, a young immigrant named Shirley Temple Wong recites her own unforgettable version:

"I pledge a lesson to the frog of the United States of America, and to the wee puppet for witches' hands. One Asian, in the vestibule, with little tea and just rice for all."

Share this passage with your students; then discuss the meaning of the real pledge and these words: *pledge, allegiance, republic, indivisible, liberty, justice.* List synonyms for each of these words on the board.

Next challenge each student to rewrite the pledge in his own words on a copy of the pattern on page 70. After students have shared their pledges, have each child glue his pattern to a red or blue sheet of paper, then cut around it to leave a border of color. Post these patterns on a bulletin board decorated with an enlarged version of the pattern on page 70. For a decorative touch, use a background of aluminum foil and a border of red-white-and-blue ribbon.

A Constitutional Learning Center

For an instant learning center that's loaded with learning opportunities, place a copy of your state's constitution and a copy of the federal Constitution at a learning center. (Call your local public library for copies of both.) Post a large Venn diagram at the center as well. During free time, let students visit the center and write ways the two documents are alike and different in the diagram.

61

Rights Versus Duties

All citizens have certain rights—such as the right to vote; and duties—such as the responsibility of paying taxes. Use this principle to help students write a class constitution. Begin by having each child list rights he thinks each student in the class should have (the right not to have his personal belongings bothered, the right to learn, etc.). Then direct students to list duties each student must fulfill to have an orderly learning environment (the duty to obey class rules, the duty not to prevent others from learning, etc.). As students share, write their responses on two large sheets of chart paper.

Post these charts; then have the class write a class constitution that incorporates the rights and duties students agree are most important. Make the constitution official by having each cooperative group discuss and vote on it, much like the state conventions had to do to approve the Constitution. When your constitution has been approved, hold a special signing ceremony. Let each student use a plumed pen (the type used at many wedding receptions) to sign a poster-sized copy of the document.

Who *Is* The Chief Justice?

Introduce students to the three branches of government established in the Constitution by decorating a bulletin board with the diagram shown below. Explain that unfortunately, few Americans can identify most of the key people elected or appointed to serve in these branches. Divide the class into groups and give each team a current almanac. Have students find the names of the following public servants:

Executive: President, Vice President, Secretary of State, Secretary of Treasury, Secretary of Defense, Attorney General
Legislative: your state's two senators, your district's representative, the Speaker of the House, President Pro Tempore of the Senate
Judicial: the names of the Supreme Court justices, including the Chief Justice

Write each person's name and job on an index card; then have students add it to the display by using a length of crepe paper to attach each card to its correct branch. For fun, ask students to poll their parents to find out how many can name the people in the list above. Tally the results; then have students tell why they think most people don't know this information.

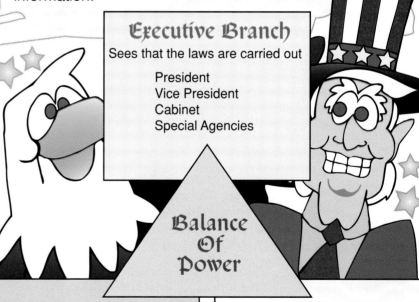

Executive Branch
Sees that the laws are carried out

President
Vice President
Cabinet
Special Agencies

Balance Of Power

Legislative Branch
Makes the laws

House of Representatives
Senate

Judicial Branch
Interprets the laws and makes sure all citizens have equal justice under the law

Supreme Court
Lesser national courts

They Spoke Out For Freedom

Roads, schools, and towns all across our country are named for individuals who spoke out for freedom. Introduce students to a sampling of these patriots with the reproducible on page 71. Remind students that these men were real human beings with the following "fast facts":

- George Washington, who was very fond of ice cream, only attended school for six years.
- John Adams was the first president to reside in the White House.
- Thomas Jefferson was a self-taught botanist. He helped dispel the popular myth that the white potato and the tomato were poisonous.
- Alexander Hamilton was the Secretary of the Treasury when he signed the Constitution. A romantic scandal destroyed his chances of becoming president.
- At 81, Benjamin Franklin was the oldest of the delegates to the Constitutional Convention. Because of the pain he experienced during bouncy carriage trips, Franklin arrived in Philadelphia in a Chinese sedan chair carried by four prisoners from the local jail.
- James Madison was so small that he was described as being "no bigger than half a piece of soap." He kept detailed notes of the entire four months and was never absent—not for a single day.

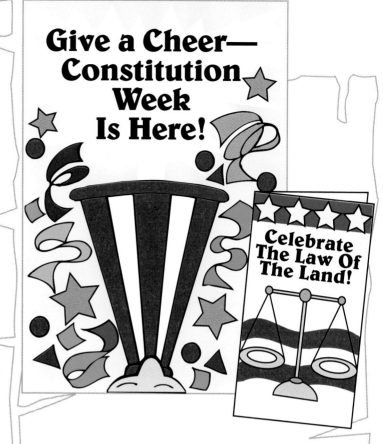

Promoting Constitution Week

Constitution Week is observed each year from September 17–23. Citizenship Day (September 17) starts the week off. Build an awareness of Constitution Week in your school with the help of your cooperative groups. Ask the class to list five important points they want the school to know about Constitution Week. For example, "The Constitution is the one main law in the United States." After everyone has agreed on the five points, assign a grade level (from grade 2 up) to each group. Have groups plan how they will make their grade level aware of Constitution Week. Suggest that students design posters, brochures, or flyers; put on a simple puppet play or skit; videotape a brief news show; make a bulletin-board display or banner; or write original poems or songs. Have groups share their ideas with the class so they can receive feedback and refine their ideas. Provide two to three class sessions during which students can prepare their materials. During Constitution Week, schedule groups to present their projects to the assigned classes.

Meet The Delegates Day

As a finishing step to the activity on the left, hold a "Meet The Delegates Day." Have each student—pretending to be the delegate he researched—wear his I.D. card and introduce himself to the other delegates. Allow students to dress in appropriate costumes. (Delegates from northern states wore their woolen suits, while southerners dressed in lighter coats and pants.) To make the session more authentic, play the role of George Washington—president of the convention—by sitting in an official chair at the front of the room. Position the student portraying James Madison nearby so he can take notes of the session, just as Madison did during the entire convention.

Before starting, pretend to lock your classroom door (every convention meeting was behind locked doors). Remind students that windows were kept closed during most sessions to discourage eavesdroppers. Since the convention was held in the heat of summer, you'll want to distribute tissues so your sweltering delegates can mop their sweaty brows during the introductions!

Finding Out About Our Founding Fathers

Introduce students to some famous and not-so-famous founding fathers who were responsible for the Constitution. Assign a convention delegate from the list below to each student. Direct the student to find out:

- the state that the delegate represented.
- whether the delegate signed the Constitution, and if not, why?
- three other interesting facts about him.

After a research period, have each student summarize her findings by completing a copy of the "Constitutional Convention I.D. Card" on page 65. Then get ready for a "Meet The Delegates Day" using the activity on the right.

Founding Fathers:

Abraham Baldwin	Alexander Hamilton
Charles Pinckney	Jonathan Dayton
Charles Cotesworth Pinckney	William Pierce
Nicholas Gilman	Elbridge Gerry
Nathaniel Gorham	William Samuel Johnson
Rufus King	John Langdon
George Mason	Robert Morris
Gouverneur Morris	Edmund Randolph
William Paterson	James Madison
Roger Sherman	William Livingston
John Dickinson	

Ramblin' Through The Preamble

At the time of its signing, many people were asking, "Why do we need a Constitution anyway?" The answers to that question are found in the preamble:

"We the People of the United States, in Order to <u>form a more perfect Union</u>, <u>establish Justice</u>, <u>insure domestic Tranquility</u>, <u>provide for the common defence</u>, <u>promote the general Welfare</u>, and <u>secure the Blessings of Liberty to ourselves and our Posterity</u>, do ordain and establish this Constitution for the United States of America."

Discuss the meanings of the underlined words and phrases; then have students complete the following activities:

- What problems led to the writing of the Constitution? Challenge each cooperative group to find out why the 13 states needed "to form a more perfect union." Then have each group write and perform a skit that tells about these problems.

- Citizens of our nation enjoy more peace on the homefront than many people of the world. Have students cut out newspaper and magazine articles that describe places around the world whose citizens are not experiencing "domestic tranquility." Post the articles; then have students discuss or write about how their lives would be affected if they traded places with the people in the articles.

- What "blessings of liberty" are you most grateful for? As a homework assignment, have each child ask five adults and/or family members this question. The next day, have students share the responses they gathered. List these on the board; then have each student draw a picture that illustrates one of the freedoms. Post these on a bulletin board titled "Blessings Of Liberty."

Pattern
Use with "Finding Out About Our Founding Fathers" on page 64.

Have each student write his information on the lines and draw or glue a picture of his founding father in the circle.

Constitutional Convention I.D. Card

Founding Father:

Student:

©1996 The Education Center, Inc. • *SEPTEMBER* • TEC198

One Letter Can Make A Difference

Encourage your students to start participating in the political process now with a letter-writing campaign. For one week, bring in copies of newspapers for students to peruse during free time. At the end of the week, have students brainstorm a list of issues they are concerned about. Then have each child write a letter to a government official expressing his concern. Remind students that one letter *can* make a difference. Eleven-year-old Grace Bedell wrote to Abraham Lincoln in 1865 asking him to grow a beard, which he did. In 1982 ten-year-old Samantha Smith wrote a letter to the leader of the Soviet Union pleading for peace. She was invited to visit the Communist country, which focused attention on the need for peace. Mail the letters using the following addresses. Included are examples of how students should start and end their letters.

The Three Branches In The News

Give students an opportunity to apply what they've learned about the three branches of government with an art project that's a snap (or snip!) to make. Have each pair of students cut out a large E (executive), L (legislative), or J (judicial) from construction paper. Provide each pair with a current newspaper; then challenge the pair to snip pictures, headlines, and captions that relate to its branch, then glue them onto its letter collage-fashion.

The President
The White House
Washington, DC 20500
Dear Mr. President:
Very respectfully yours,

(U.S. Senator)
The Honorable Mary Jones
United States Senate
Washington, DC 20510
Dear Senator Jones:
Sincerely yours,

The Vice President
The White House
Washington, DC 20500
Dear Mr. Vice President:
Very respectfully yours,

(Member of the President's Cabinet)
The Honorable Robert Smith
The Secretary of Defense
Washington, DC 20301
Dear Mr. Secretary
(or Dear Madam Secretary):
Sincerely yours,

(U.S. Representative)
The Honorable Thomas Martin
House of Representatives
Washington, DC 20515
Dear Mr. Martin:
Sincerely yours,

Justice Brown Retires
Courts Are Busy!
Case Goes to Court

A Right Or A Crime?

One of the most familiar symbols of our country and its government is the American flag. During the Vietnam War, activists were arrested for burning the flag as a way to protest the war. The Supreme Court ruled in 1990 that flag burning was a form of symbolic speech protected by the First Amendment. What do your students think—should flag burning be a crime? Have each child pretend to be a justice on the Supreme Court. Tell students that the issue of flag burning has just been brought before the court. Each justice must state his/her opinion and give at least three reasons for that opinion. Have students write their opinions, then share them with the other justices in their cooperative groups.

Electing A Class Mascot

Give students a hands-on lesson in the democratic process with the following activity:

1. Ask each student to submit a drawing of a mascot he would like to represent your class. Be sure the student labels his drawing with the mascot's name and his name. Display the pictures.
2. Explain that in order to elect a class mascot, a general election must be held. Only registered voters will be allowed to participate. Choose one student to be the registrar. Set aside one day for students to register to vote.
3. Explain that now the ballot must be filled. Encourage students to circulate petitions for their favorite choices. On each petition, the student should list the candidate's name and a short recommendation. Decide in advance how many signatures will qualify a candidate for the ballot and whether students may sign multiple petitions.
4. Post a list of the candidates who qualified to be on the ballot. Then have each student write a one- to three-minute campaign speech for the candidate of his choice. Encourage the student to make a bumper sticker, placard, or poster to display on the podium while he speaks.
5. Provide time for each student to give his speech.
6. Hold an election.
7. Tabulate the votes and announce the winner. Have students compare the steps in this activity with those for an actual presidential election.

VOTE for Dweedle!

He'll be an out-of-this-world mascot!

Make Mine Dweedle!

E Pluribus what?

Create A Currency

Once students have studied different forms of currency with the activity on the left, let them become mint masters and create their own currencies. Have students follow these steps:

1. Select a shape for a quarter, a $1 bill, and a $5 bill. Who said coins must always be round and bills must always be rectangular?
2. On scrap paper, design your coin and bills. Sketch a seal to place on each coin/bill. Also decide on a mint mark, a motto, a secret code phrase (similar to *E Pluribus Unum*), and a date of issue. Include the denomination and "United States of America" somewhere on each coin/bill.
3. Choose three famous persons to picture on your quarter, $1 bill, and $5 bill.
4. Draw the coin and the two bills. Then cut them out and decorate the backs.
5. Write a short press release informing the public of your brand-new currency and telling why it is an improvement over the current currency.

Minting And Moolah

The Constitution grants Congress the power to mint money. Give each cooperative group a $1 bill, a half-dollar, a quarter, a dime, a nickel, a penny, and a magnifying glass. Have students examine the bill and coins to find common characteristics. Share the following information about our currency:

- Mint marks often appear on coins, almost hidden in the design. A small capital letter *D* indicates the coin was minted in Denver; an *S* indicates San Francisco, while a coin with no mark was minted in Philadelphia.
- The penny has always been copper except during 1943. The war created a copper shortage, so pennies were made from steel instead.
- The Latin phrase *E Pluribus Unum* is printed on all coins. It means "out of many, one" and refers to the creation of the United States from the 13 original colonies.
- Most $1 bills wear out after about 18 months in circulation.
- All U.S. money carries the nation's official motto, *In God We Trust.*

After sharing this information, challenge each student to create his own currency in the following activity.

Buffalo Bill

Name That Amendment

When first written, some of the delegates feared the Constitution did not say enough about the rights of individual citizens. So ten amendments, called the Bill of Rights, were added. The form below outlines the basic rights listed in the Bill of Rights, but in language your students can understand. After students have had a chance to learn about the Bill of Rights, play a fun game of Name That Amendment. Divide your class into teams of four or five students each. Give each team a copy of the outline below and ten cards labeled one to ten. One at a time, read a phrase listed on the right. Give teams time to discuss their answers; then have each team's captain hold up the correct amendment card. Award a point for each correct answer.

Phrases (amendment in parentheses)

- may worship as we please (1)
- freedom of the press (1)
- may gather peaceably (1)
- may speak openly about what we think and feel (1)
- can't be punished for religious beliefs (1)
- may keep guns (2)
- soldiers can't be placed in our homes during peacetime (3)
- no unreasonable searches (4)
- warrants needed by police (4)
- can't be tried twice for the same crime (5)
- freedom from testifying against oneself (5)
- trial by jury (5)
- entitled to a speedy trial (6)
- right to have a lawyer (6)
- right to have witnesses to testify in your defense (6)
- laws must be followed in noncriminal trials (7)
- innocent until proven guilty (8)
- prevents bail that is too high (8)
- forbids unfair fines (8)
- forbids cruel and unusual punishment (8)
- states and people have additional rights (9)
- federal government only has powers given to it in the Constitution (10)

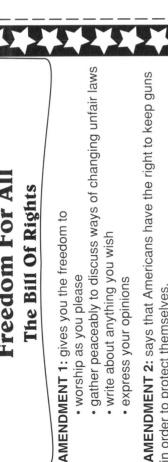

Freedom For All
The Bill Of Rights

AMENDMENT 1: gives you the freedom to
- worship as you please
- gather peaceably to discuss ways of changing unfair laws
- write about anything you wish
- express your opinions

AMENDMENT 2: says that Americans have the right to keep guns in order to protect themselves.

AMENDMENT 3: says that soldiers may not be placed in your home during times of peace.

AMENDMENT 4: prevents officials from searching you or your home without first receiving permission from a judge.

AMENDMENTS 5, 6, 7, and 8: discuss the rights of a person who has been accused of a crime. These rights include:
- the right to a fair and speedy trial
- the right to have your case decided by a jury
- the right to decide not to testify against yourself
- the right to be told what crime you supposedly have committed
- the right to see and hear the people who have accused you
- the right to have a lawyer

These amendments also protect innocent people from staying in jail until they have had their trials. Fines cannot be too high. And punishment cannot be cruel or unusual.

AMENDMENT 9: says that all rights not listed in the Constitution or the Bill of Rights belong to the people. It also says that the government cannot deny those rights to any person.

AMENDMENT 10: says that the federal government may have only the powers given to it by the Constitution. Any other powers belong to the states and to the people.

Patterns

Use with the bulletin board on page 61. Enlarge the Uncle Sam pattern. Attach a strip of bulletin-board paper, cut to resemble a long banner, to the flagpole (see the illustration on page 61).

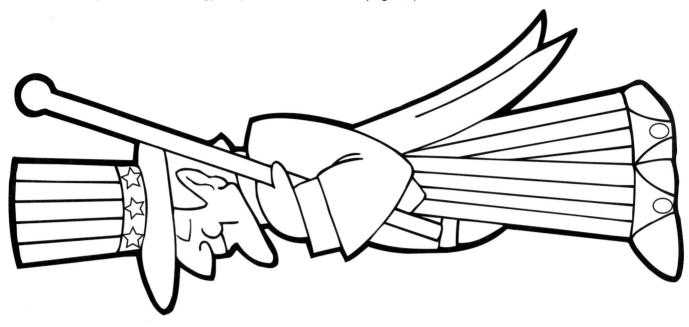

Research, creative thinking

Speaking Out For Freedom

These famous men all worked to make sure that the United States would be a nation of freedom for all. Research each man. In his speech bubble, write what you think each patriot might say about his role in making America the "land of the free."

Alexander Hamilton

George Washington

James Madison

John Adams

Thomas Jefferson

Benjamin Franklin

Bonus Box: Research to find out which two men above didn't attend the Constitutional Convention. Why didn't they attend? Write your answer on the back of this page.

©1996 The Education Center, Inc. • *SEPTEMBER* • TEC198 • Key p. 95

Note To The Teacher: Use with "They Spoke Out For Freedom" on page 63. You may wish to pair up students to complete this activity.

71

Name _____ *Contract*

Framing The Constitution

In 1787, 55 men met in Philadelphia. Their job? To draw up plans for how to run the new nation called the United States. These "framers of the Constitution" met for four months. They argued. They debated. They worried. But they finally agreed on a plan called the Constitution. It was approved by nine of the states by June 21, 1788.

Directions: Learn more about these men, their meetings, and the Constitution by choosing _____ of the activities below. Complete these activities by _____.

• Research the history of your state's ratification of the Constitution. Write your information vertically on a large index card. Write your name and the title of your report vertically on another card. Draw an illustration (also vertically) on a third card. Then tape the edges of the cards together to make a standing triangular report. Display it on a table for others to read.

• Draw a political cartoon that might have been in a Philadelphia newspaper during the Constitutional Convention. Glue the cartoon on a colorful piece of construction paper; then staple it to a bulletin board.

• Be a framer of the Constitution! On a piece of white paper, use a fountain pen to copy the preamble to the Constitution. Use your best cursive handwriting. Sign the paper. Ask several friends to add their signatures too. Then use Popsicle® sticks, twigs, cardboard, and any other material to make a unique frame for your preamble.

• Read parts of the Constitution. Then write a quiz that includes ten questions you think every American citizen should be able to answer. Make a key. Give your test to five adults. How did they do?

• Write a skit about the first meeting of the Constitutional Convention. Ask several friends, your parents, or other family members to take the roles in your skit. Then tape-record your skit to make a radio play. Don't forget sound effects!

• Draw a portrait of the Constitutional delegate you think is most interesting or most important. On an index card, write a paragraph telling why you chose this person. Attach the card to the portrait.

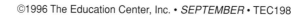

Note To The Teacher: Fill in the blanks above before duplicating. These tasks are also great activities for the whole class or for small groups to complete.

★ ★ ★ ★ ★ The First Thirteen ★ ★ ★ ★ ★

Part 1: Read each clue. In the first blank, write the name of the state. In the second blank, write its number on the map.

a. I sent no delegates to the convention. I was the last of the 13 states to approve the Constitution.
_____ _____

b. The Constitutional Convention was held in one of my cities. Ben Franklin was one of my most famous residents. _____ _____

c. A famous compromise made between the big and little states was named for me. I was the fifth state to approve the Constitution. _____ _____

d. I was the smallest state to attend the Convention. I was first to approve the Constitution.
_____ _____

e. George Washington and James Madison both served as my delegates.
_____ _____

f. I led the small states with a plan (named for me). It called for equal representation in both the Senate and the House. _____ _____

g. The Constitution was ratified when I voted *yes* on June 21, 1788.
_____ _____

h. I was the southernmost state and was fourth to approve the Constitution.
_____ _____

i. I am an agricultural state that depended on slavery. I first voted *no*, but changed my mind later and voted *yes.* _____ _____

j. My delegates included Charles Pinckney and his cousin, also named Charles Pinckney! I voted *yes* on May 23, 1788. _____ _____

k. I am sandwiched between Virginia and Pennsylvania. I approved the Constitution on April 28, 1788.
_____ _____

l. I am home to Plymouth Rock. I approved the Constitution on February 6, 1788.
_____ _____

m. Alexander Hamilton was my delegate after John Lansing, Jr., and Robert Yates walked out. _____ _____

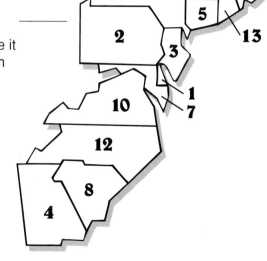

Part 2: Color blue the states that approved the Constitution before it was ratified. Color yellow the states that approved the Constitution after it had been ratified.

Dates of Ratification			
Map No.	**Date**	**Map No.**	**Date**
1	12/7/1787	8	5/23/1788
2	12/12/1787	9	6/21/1788
3	12/18/1787	10	6/25/1788
4	1/2/1788	11	7/26/1788
5	1/9/1788	12	11/21/1789
6	2/6/1788	13	5/29/1790
7	4/28/1788		

NATIVE AMERICANS: HONORING THEIR HERITAGE

Native American Day is celebrated on the last Friday of September. This special day honors the contributions of North America's Native Americans. Investigate the diverse cultures and heritage of Native Americans with the following learning-packed activities.

A TIME TO CELEBRATE?

To people of European descent, Christopher Columbus's historic voyage was a magnificent event that led to the discovery of North America. But to many Native Americans, Columbus represents the beginning of an era that altered the Indian way of life forever. Whose perspective is correct? Could both be correct? After discussing the two perspectives, divide the class into groups. Have each group divide a piece of chart paper in half. On the top half of the paper, have students list reasons why many people celebrate Columbus Day. On the other half, have students list reasons why others—including many Native Americans—don't celebrate this day. Point out the two sides of this issue; then ask each student to reflect on a disagreement she has had and to write about the conflict from her perspective. Then have her write about the problem from the point of view of the other person(s) involved. Discuss how trying to see things through someone else's eyes can help to resolve a conflict.

HOME SWEET HOME

Homes are a direct result of the type of environment that surrounds a people. In the case of Native Americans, homes also reflected their belief systems and social structure. Use the reproducible on page 83 to introduce students to the variety of Native American homes. After students have played the Concentration-style game, discuss why different regional tribes built certain types of homes (the climate, natural resources, etc.). Then include this information in a variation of the game. On each nonpicture card, direct students to list the materials used to make that particular home. Have students play the game again, adding a new rule that a player can only keep a match if he can state a reason why the tribe built that style of shelter.

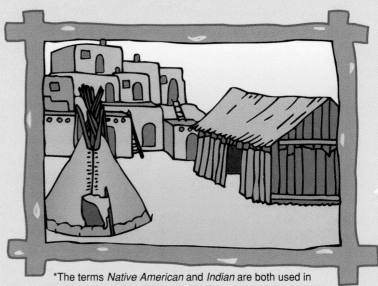

*The terms *Native American* and *Indian* are both used in this unit. Explain to students that Christopher Columbus —upon reaching the New World—mistakenly thought that he had reached the Indies and so named its inhabitants *Indians*. The word *Indian* was not in the vocabulary of Native Americans since almost every tribe had its own name. Today many Indians refer to themselves as Native Americans.

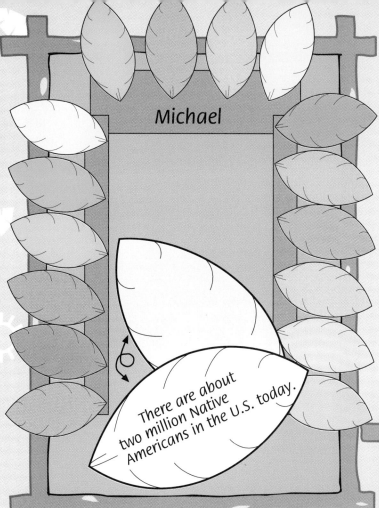

Michael

There are about two million Native Americans in the U.S. today.

STORY STICKS

Many Native American tribes used pictures, symbols, and storytelling to document their lives. For example, Arizona's Pima Indians used story sticks to tell about their adventures. Each smooth, flat stick was decorated with pictures that symbolized important events.

Challenge students to make story sticks of their lives. Have each child list four major events or details about his life on paper; then have him draw a picture or symbol to represent each event. Next have the student use markers or paints to draw his pictures on a wooden paint-stirring stick. For a finishing touch, have the student staple a few feathers (from a craft store) to a strip of fabric, then tie the strip around his stick. *(For another story-stick idea, see page 77.)*

FINE-FEATHERED FACTS

Like many people, your students may think that the feathered war bonnet was worn by all Native Americans of the past. Explain that headdresses were different for each tribe and that some did not wear them at all. The war bonnet was worn by Plains Indians such as the Comanche and the Sioux.

Let students create an ongoing display that grows as you study Native Americans. Give each child a 3" x 9" strip of brown paper to color and label with his name. Attach a long strip of brown paper to each end of the headband; then staple the headband to a bulletin board. Duplicate the feather pattern on page 84. Each time a student learns a fascinating fact about Native Americans, let him color and cut out a feather. Then have him label the back of the feather with the fact and attach it to his headband (fact side down). By the end of the unit, each student will have a colorful headdress representing all he's learned about Native Americans.

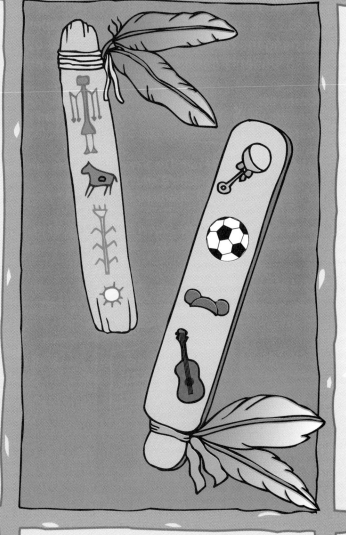

MYTHS AND LEGENDS

Native American literature is rich in colorful legends that explain the world and nature. Read aloud some Native American tales that explain natural phenomena such as how the moon was created (see the resource list below). Explain that even though these phenomena can be explained scientifically, the myths help us learn about Native American beliefs and cultures.

After reading several stories, give each pair of students one of these topics:

volcanoes	earthquakes	constellations
mountains	rain	tornadoes
hail	sunrise/sunset	snow
rainbows	moon	comets

Have each pair research and write a one-page report about the scientific facts behind its topic. Then have the students write a brief myth or legend that explains the phenomenon in a manner similar to the Native American tales they have read. Have each pair mount its writings back-to-back on a piece of construction paper. Then hang the projects from your ceiling at eye level so students can flip them back and forth.

Resource list:

Thirteen Moons On Turtle's Back: A Native American Year Of Moons retold by Joseph Bruchac & Jonathan London

The Woman Who Fell From The Sky: The Iroquois Story Of Creation retold by John Bierhorst

The First Strawberries: A Cherokee Story retold by Joseph Bruchac

How The Stars Fell Into The Sky: A Navajo Legend by Jerrie Oughton

DISEASE: THE SILENT KILLER

It is estimated that between 7 and 15 million Native Americans lived on North America when Columbus touched its shores in 1492. By 1900 there were only 250,000 Indians left. What happened? Though many Native American lives were lost fighting for their land, many more millions died from diseases brought by the white man from Europe. Help students visualize these staggering and sad statistics with the reproducible math activity on page 85. After students complete the sheet, discuss with them the effect this drastic change in population would have on the Native American culture.

RESEARCH STORY STICKS

The diversity of Native Americans is tied to the varied regions in which they lived. To help students understand this diversity, give each child a copy of page 86. (Or make a transparency to display on an overhead projector.) Have students note the different tribes listed for each region on the map. Point out that the stereotypical Native American symbols—tepee, war bonnet, buffalo, etc.—represent only a small group of Indians who lived in the Plains region. Have each cooperative group research one of the tribes listed on the map. Post these questions for groups to answer as they research:

- Where did the tribe live?
- How was the tribe organized and governed?
- What type of clothing did the people wear?
- What types of food did they eat?
- What types of shelter did they use?
- What made the tribe different from other Native American groups?
- Where is the tribe today?

After students have completed their research, have each group complete the following steps to create a giant story stick (similar to the story stick described on page 75) detailing its research.

Making The Research Story Stick:
1. Divide a large piece of poster board into eight horizontal, equal-sized sections.
2. Write the name of your tribe in the top section.
3. In each remaining section, answer one of the research questions posted. Include an illustration or symbol in each section.
4. Bend the poster board into a cylindrical shape; then tape the edges together with clear tape.
5. Cut out a circular cap for each end of your cylinder from construction paper. Tape each cap to an end of the cylinder, using clear tape.
6. Staple several real or paper feathers to a long strip of thick yarn or fabric. Tie the strip around one end of your research stick.

DIG THIS!

Buried under the earth is a storehouse of knowledge about the lifestyle, beliefs, and customs of Native Americans. Discuss with students how archaeologists read history by digging up and examining *artifacts* (items made by humans long ago). Show students a rock and ask, "Is this an artifact?" Students should conclude that since the stone was not made by a human, it's not an artifact. Next tie the rock to a stick and ask the same question. Students should conclude that since the stone has been fashioned into a tool by human hands, it could now be considered an artifact. Follow up this discussion by having students complete the "Dig This!" reproducible on page 88.

BUFFALO AND THE PLAINS INDIANS

Native Americans who lived on the Great Plains used the limited natural resources of their environment efficiently and effectively. For example, almost every part of the buffalo had at least one use. As buffalo herds were massacred by the white man, the damage done to the Plains Indians and their culture was staggering.

Help students grasp the importance of the buffalo to the Plains Indians' culture with the reproducible on page 87. Before distributing the sheet, explain that the buffalo was like a general store to the Plains Indians because they could use its parts to meet many basic needs. Let students complete the activity individually, in pairs, or in groups. After revealing the answers (page 96), invite students to write summaries in which they explain how losing the buffalo harmed the Plains Indians' culture and lifestyle.

OWNER STICKS

To show ownership, we put our names on items. Native Americans of the Great Plains used another method instead. The *owner stick* was a straight piece of birch that was uniquely decorated to convey a family's history or name. If a family had killed a deer and needed to leave the kill, they would leave their family's owner stick by the remains. This showed anyone passing by that the kill belonged to someone.

As a unique homework assignment, challenge each student to use available materials to make an owner stick that will represent his family without using words. Students may use an actual stick, a paper cutout, a wooden dowel, or any other handy item. Have each student transport his stick to school in a paper bag. The next day, pull each stick from its bag and have the class guess the owner's identity.

TAKE A CHANCE WITH BASKET DICE

Most Native American games were either games of chance or games of dexterity. The most common Native American game of chance used a bundle of sticks that included one marked or painted stick. A player would divide the bundle in half and hold each half in a hand. His opponent would guess which hand held the marked stick. Play this stick game that incorporates simple math skills:

To prepare the game: Give each pair of students five tongue depressors. On two of the sticks, have the students draw a star on one side and a crescent moon on the other. On the remaining three sticks, have the students completely color one side with black crayon while leaving the other side blank. Place these dice into a shoebox along with 50 toothpicks.

To play the game: Give each player 25 toothpicks. The first player tosses the dice out of the box onto the table. If he has one of the following combinations, he earns that number of points (toothpicks):

- 2 moons and 3 uncolored sides = 10 toothpicks from opponent
- 2 stars and 3 black sides = 10 toothpicks from opponent
- 1 moon, 1 star, and 3 uncolored sides = 1 toothpick from opponent
- 1 moon, 1 star, and 3 black sides = 1 toothpick from opponent

All other combinations do not earn any points.

Players alternate turns until one player runs out of toothpicks or time is up. The winner is the player with the most toothpicks.

A math tie-in: Before students play the game, have them list all the possible combinations of dice that could happen on a single turn. (The list should show 12 possible combinations.) Have each pair list these 12 combinations; then have them keep a tally of which ones are tossed during a game. After the game, compile a class tally of the combinations that appeared. Have students see if there is a pattern or if one combination appeared more frequently than others.

SHELLING OUT MONEY

Like other Native Americans, the Eastern Woodlands Indians did not have currency like we use today. Instead, they traded *wampum*. These white and purple beads—made from clamshells—were strung together to make intricately patterned bands.

Introduce students to wampum with this hypothetical situation: You're walking down the street and see two bills—$1 and $100—on the ground. You can pick up only one bill. Which will you choose? Students will likely respond in favor of the $100 bill. Next show them a real $1 bill and a $100 bill of play money. Now which would they choose? Discuss with the class what makes money valuable. Point out that the Native Americans agreed that wampum was valuable, and thus these beads were used as currency. Extend this discussion by having students complete the reproducible graphing activity on page 89.

NAME-CALLING OR JUST A NAME?

Sports teams have often chosen names that to many people reflect Native American stereotypes (Atlanta Braves, Golden State Warriors, Washington Redskins, etc.). Recently some schools and colleges have changed their team names. For example, the Marquette Warriors are now the Marquette Golden Eagles. But other schools and teams don't agree that these types of names are harmful.

Have students examine sources such as newspapers and sports magazines to find team names that have a Native American slant. Compile a class list. Then have each student divide the list into three categories: Positive Connotation, Negative Connotation, or Neutral Connotation. Have students share reasons for their categorizations. For example, one student may think that "Braves" has the positive connotation of courage. Another may think "Redskins" is negative because it refers to a stereotypical skin color. A neutral connotation may be "Seminole" since it's the name of an actual tribe. Point out that the mascots and logos used by a team may be negative even if the team name is neutral. Have the class choose one of the teams listed; then hold a contest to rename the team and create a new mascot and logo.

EXPLORERS AND NATIVE AMERICANS

Combining a study of explorers with a unit on Native Americans is a natural fit since these two groups are closely connected in history. Divide your class in half; then assign each child to research either a famous North American explorer or a Native American (see the lists that follow). Have those students who are researching explorers focus on their treatment of Native Americans and its effects. Direct students who are researching famous Native Americans to find out why their subjects became famous. Have each student compile his information in a brief biographical sketch; then pair each explorer researcher with a Native American researcher. Have the pair tell each other about their famous persons. *(For a way to display these reports, see the bulletin-board idea that follows.)*

EXPLORERS:
Hispanic explorers: See the list on page 90.
French explorers: Jacques Cartier, Samuel de
  Champlain, Louis Joliet and Jacques Marquette,
  Robert La Salle
English explorers: John Cabot (an Italian who sailed for
  the British), Sir Walter Raleigh, Henry Hudson (who
  sailed for the Dutch)

NATIVE AMERICANS:

Chief Joseph	Massasoit	Montezuma
Geronimo	Pocahontas	Pontiac
Powhatan	Quanah	Red Cloud
John Ross	Sacagawea	Sequoya
Sitting Bull	Tecumseh	Jim Thorpe
Susan La Flesche	Sara Winnemucca	Osceola
Picotte		

He was born in a Creek Indian village.

He joined the Seminole tribe.

He led the Seminoles in the Second Seminole War.

DOORS OF DISTINCTION

To display the student-written biographies completed in the activity above, have each student cut a piece of poster board slightly larger than his report. Then have him rubber cement two 1" x 2" poster-board strips to the left side of the poster board and draw a doorknob on the right side. Direct the student to write three clues about his person (without identifying him/her by name) on the poster board. Staple each poster-board door to the board at the tabs; then staple the completed report behind the door. Close each door by pinning it to the board with a pushpin. During free time, let students open each door and meet the famous person inside by reading the report.

1. Cut a piece of poster board in half length-wise. Draw your group's illustrations on the strip in the middle area (see the diagram).

2. Bring the two short ends together so that the illustrations are on the outside of the resulting drum. Attach the ends together with transparent tape.
3. Using a pencil, lightly trace one end of the drum onto paper. Then draw another line around the outside of the tracing to make a slightly larger circle.
4. Draw four large triangles on the perimeter of the larger circle as shown.
5. Cut out the larger circle with the triangles attached. Decorate this drumhead with the name of your ceremony, the name of the tribe(s) who performed it, and the region in which the tribe(s) lived.

The Sun Dance

CEREMONIES: DRUMMING UP A GREAT REPORT!

Ceremonies were a vital part of everyday life for all Native American tribes. They were a way to celebrate births and marriages, give thanks to or ask the gods for favors, initiate members into secret societies, or prepare for a war or a hunt. Each regional Native American group had its own unique ceremonies. For example, Indians of the Southeast held an annual green corn festival to celebrate a new harvest.

Since drums were an important part of many ceremonies, let your students drum up some fascinating facts about this topic. Assign a region from the list on page 86 to each cooperative group. Instruct each group to find out about one important ceremony celebrated by Native Americans who lived in its region; then direct each group to draw four sketches that illustrate its information. When these sketches are ready, have groups complete the following steps to make a related project that can't be beat!

6. Place the drumhead on the top of the drum; then fold the triangular tabs downward so they rest on the side of the drum without covering the pictures.
7. Poke a small hole through each triangular tab and the drum. Also poke a hole near the bottom of the drum directly under each tab.
8. For each tab, string a length of yarn through the holes. Tie the ends of the yarn together on the inside of the drum.
9. After describing your ceremony to the class, display the drum on a table.

NATIVE AMERICAN SHELTER GAME

Native Americans living in different regions of North America had their own ways of building shelters. How they designed their homes depended on the climate of their region, the building materials that were available, how often the tribe moved, and their religious beliefs. Below are nine types of Native American homes. After examining them, pair up with a partner and play the Native American Shelter Game!

To make the game:
1. Get nine index cards. On each card, copy the caption listed under one home.
2. Get nine more index cards. Cut out the pictures of the homes (without the captions) from one copy of this page. Glue each to an index card.
3. Write "Answer Key" at the top of the other copy of this page.

To play the game:
1. Shuffle the 18 cards; then place them facedown in a 3 x 6 grid.
2. Player One turns over two cards. If the cards match (picture and caption), he keeps both cards and takes another turn. If they don't match, he turns the cards back over, and Player Two takes a turn. Check matches by looking at your Answer Key page.
3. The player with the most cards at the end of the game is the winner.

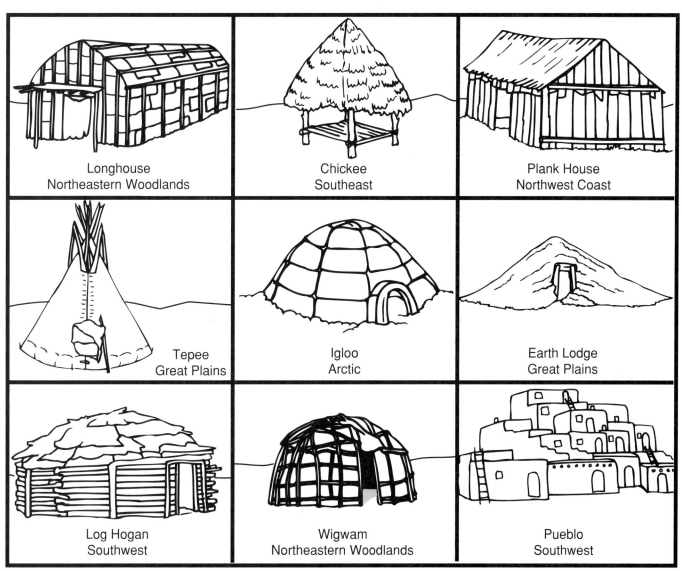

Longhouse Northeastern Woodlands	Chickee Southeast	Plank House Northwest Coast
Tepee Great Plains	Igloo Arctic	Earth Lodge Great Plains
Log Hogan Southwest	Wigwam Northeastern Woodlands	Pueblo Southwest

Note To The Teacher: Use with "Home Sweet Home" on page 74. Provide each student with a copy of this page. Provide each pair of students with scissors, glue, and 18 small index cards.

Pattern
Use with "Fine-Feathered Facts" on page 75.

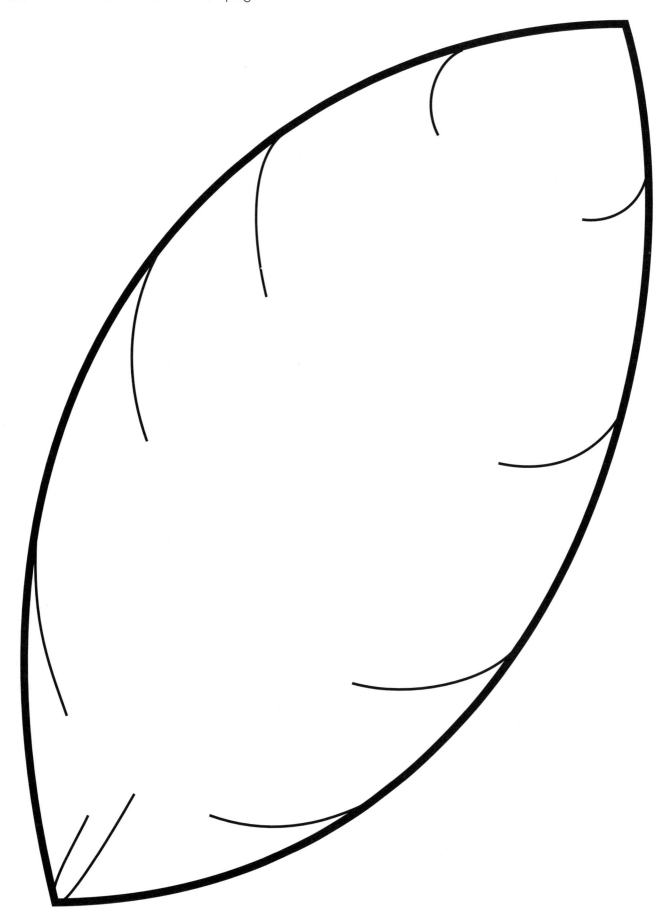

NUMBERS PAINT THE PICTURE

Christopher Columbus first touched North America's shores in 1492. Historians think that as many as 15 million Native Americans lived in North America at that time. By the end of 1900, there were only 250,000 Native Americans in North America. What happened? Many Native Americans died from diseases brought to the New World by Europeans. By 1990, the Native American population had risen to about two million.

Directions: Use the information below to complete each graph.

1492:	15,000,000	Native Americans
1900:	250,000	Native Americans
1990:	2,000,000	Native Americans

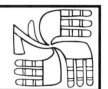

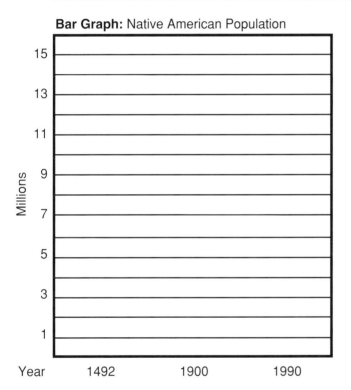

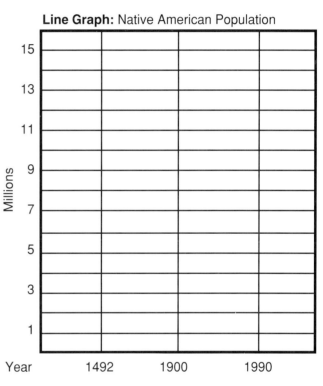

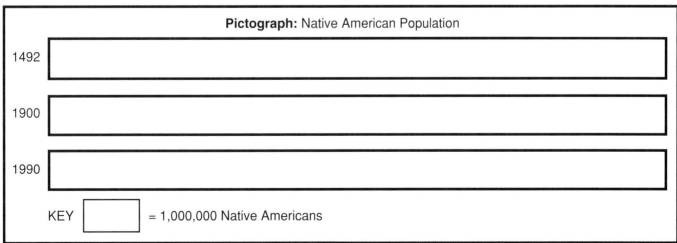

Answer on the back of this page: Why do graphs make it easier to understand statistics like the ones in the box above?

Note To The Teacher: Use with "Disease: The Silent Killer" on page 76.

NATIVE AMERICAN CULTURE AREAS

Below is a map that shows some of the major regions, or *culture areas,* in which Native Americans lived long ago. Tribes living in the same region were alike in some ways; but in other ways they were different.

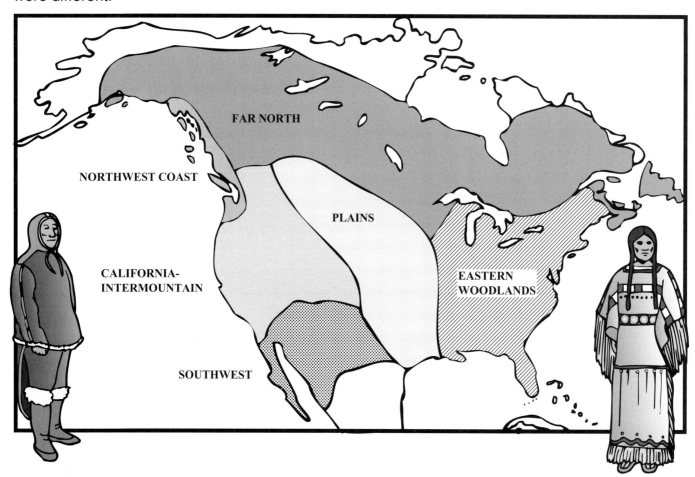

Northwest Coast
Tlingit
Haida
Klikitat

California-Intermountain
Pomo
Maidu
Paiute
Shoshone
Ute
Nez Percé

Southwest
Apache
Navajo
Pueblo
Hopi

Plains
Arapaho
Cheyenne
Pawnee
Sioux
Comanche
Mandan
Crow

Eastern Woodlands
Iroquois
Huron
Seneca
Shawnee
Cherokee
Chickasaw
Seminole

Far North
Chippewa
Cree
Algonquin

Note To The Teacher: Use with "Research Story Sticks" on page 77 and "Ceremonies: Drumming Up A Great
Report!" on page 82.

THE BUFFALO MALL

Native Americans who lived on the Great Plains depended on the buffalo for most of their needs. They had at least one use—and sometimes more—for almost every part of the animal.

Directions: Welcome to "Buffalo Mall"! Look at the list of buffalo parts below. Decide which part was used to make each necessity listed in the stores below; then write the letter of the part in the blank. Some necessities may have more than one letter in the blank. Happy shopping!

A. soft hide*	F. stomach contents	K. teeth	P. fat
B. rawhide*	G. bones	L. blood	Q. hair/fur
C. tail	H. tendons	M. horns	R. liver
D. dung	I. hooves	N. ribs	S. backbone
E. gall bladder	J. brains	O. tongue	

*Rawhide was hairless, tough, waterproof buffalo hide that hadn't been tanned. It was used to make tougher and heavier things like cooking pots. Soft hide was tanned with the hair on and was used for clothing or blankets.

Clothes R Here
____ mittens
____ coat/robe
____ dress
____ belt
____ leggings
____ necklace

Feet First Shoe Store
____ moccasins
____ laces
____ shoe soles

Feel Better Pharmacy
____ medicine
____ diapers
____ flyswatter

Arts & Crafts Shack
____ paints
____ brushes
____ tanning oil

Groceries Galore
____ pudding
____ soup
____ cold cuts

Beauty-Mart
____ hair gloss
____ hairbrush
____ soap
____ makeup

Sporting Spot
____ arrows
____ bow
____ shield
____ club
____ knife

Toys & More
____ doll
____ ball
____ dice
____ top
____ rattle

The Transportation Depot
____ dogsled
____ toboggan
____ boat
____ saddle

Kitchen Corner
____ water container
____ spoons
____ bowl
____ food storage bin
____ fuel for fires

Note To The Teacher: Use with "Buffalo And The Plains Indians" on page 78. For an answer key and additional information to share with students, see page 96.

DIG THIS!

Archaeologists are people who study early cultures by looking at things they left behind. An archaeologist chooses a small area which she thinks might contain buried *artifacts*. (An *artifact* is something made by a human being.) Then she covers the area with a grid made of string. The grid is numbered and labeled like the one below. When an archaeologist finds an artifact, she labels it with a number and letter according to where she found it. Later she uses a picture of the grid to identify where the artifact was found.

Directions: Here is a picture of a Native American archaeology site. Draw conclusions about the Native American artifacts found here by answering the questions below. Use the back of this page if you need more space.

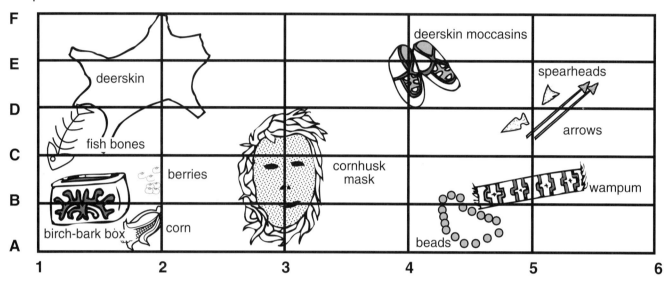

1. What artifact did you find at E-2? _____ What can you conclude about this tribe from the artifact? _____.

2. What coordinates tell you where to find the cornhusk mask? _____
   What does the mask tell you about the culture of these Native Americans? _____
   _____.

3. What part of the site was where the people probably prepared their food? _____
   _____.
   What types of food did these people eat? _____
   _____.

4. What material might these people have used to make clothing? _____
   _____ What helped you come to this
   conclusion? _____
   _____.

5. Did these Native Americans trade with each other or other people? _____
   How do you know? _____.

Bonus Box: Create your own archaeological site! Research a Native American group. Then draw a grid like the one above. Draw artifacts belonging to your tribe in the grid. On another piece of paper, describe each artifact, its location on the grid, and what it tells about your Native American group.

MAKING A WAMPUM BELT

Make your own wampum belt by following these directions:

Materials: 100 strips of white paper (1/2" x 8 1/2")   pencil and scissors
20 pieces of string (each 10" long)   clear tape
10 x 10 square of graph paper (100 squares)   purple marker

To make wampum beads:

1. Using your purple marker, color squares on your graph paper to make a pattern of white and purple blocks.

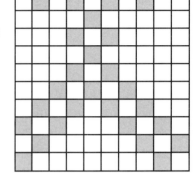

2. Count the number of squares: _____ purple; _____ white.

3. For every purple square in your grid, color a paper strip with the purple marker (one side only). Set aside the remaining white strips, making sure you have one for each of your white blocks.

4. Wrap each strip of paper tightly around a pencil as shown (purple side out for the purple strips). Tape the end of the strip with clear tape; then slide your bead off the pencil.

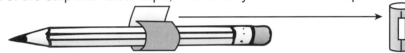

5. Look at the first horizontal row of squares on your graph paper. On your desk, make a row of beads that matches that row of squares. See the example.

Row #1

6. Take the first bead in the row and slip it on a string. Loop the string around the bead as shown and knot it. Now string the remaining beads in that row in order until you come to the end of the row.

7. Loop the string around the last bead in the row and knot it just like you did in step 6. Place this finished row of beads carefully on your desk.

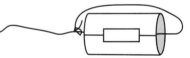

8. Repeat steps 5–7 for each of the other nine rows in your graph. Work carefully so you string your beads in the proper order.

To make the wampum belt:

1. Line up all 10 strings of beads in order to match your graph-paper design.
2. Tie a piece of string to the last row where shown. Weave the string through the rows between the first two columns of beads, using an over-and-under method. When you get to the top of the design, tie the weaving string to the top row.
3. Repeat step 2 for the remaining eight columns.
4. Trim any extra string.

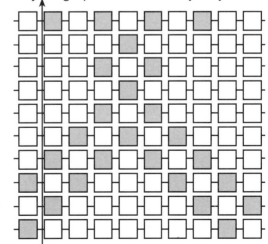

Note To The Teacher: Use with "Shelling Out Money" on page 80. Before completing the activity, explain the concept of wampum to students, including the fact that purple beads were considered the most valuable. Break this project into several sessions. Provide each student with a small manila envelope in which to store his supplies between sessions.

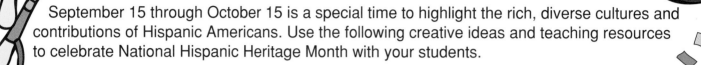

Celebrating National Hispanic Heritage Month

September 15 through October 15 is a special time to highlight the rich, diverse cultures and contributions of Hispanic Americans. Use the following creative ideas and teaching resources to celebrate National Hispanic Heritage Month with your students.

Hispanic America: A Brief Introduction

Hispanic Americans—often called *Latinos*—make up the fastest-growing minority in the United States. According to the 1990 U.S. census, 22.4 million people identified themselves as Hispanic. Hispanics contribute to life in the United States in every possible profession—from migrant workers who work the fields to astronauts in outer space.

Hispanic Americans is a broad category. The term *Hispanic* refers to anyone with ancestors who can be traced back to Spain. However, Hispanics are more likely to call themselves Mexicans, Puerto Ricans, Cubans, Argentineans, etc. There are similarities among the various cultures, but they are not exactly alike. Hispanic Americans have added their own uniqueness to the hodgepodge of races and nationalities that we call America.

Discovering The Americas

Christopher Columbus, an Italian navigator sailing in ships provided by Spain, discovered the New World. Soon Spanish conquistadors followed, searching for gold, jewels, and—in the case of Juan Ponce de León—a Fountain of Youth. Spanish exploration and colonization resulted in the spread of Christianity and a mixing of cultures that forever changed the face of the Americas.

Provide each pair of students with a 9" x 12" sheet of white construction paper. Assign each pair an explorer from the list below to research. With the paper turned horizontally, have the pair write a paragraph describing the explorer's adventures across the bottom third of the sheet. Also have the pair illustrate an important accomplishment attributed to the explorer. When all of the reports have been completed, display them end to end to make a timeline, with students determining the correct chronological order of their projects.

Christopher Columbus (sailing for Spain)
Juan Ponce de León
Álvar Núñez Cabeza de Vaca
Hernando de Soto
Vasco Núñez de Balboa
Hernando Cortés
Francisco Vásquez de Coronado
Pedro Menéndez de Avilés
Estevanico
Pedro de Alvarado
Francisco Pizarro

Christopher Columbus was an Italian who sailed for Spain. He was the first European to reach Latin America, in 1492.

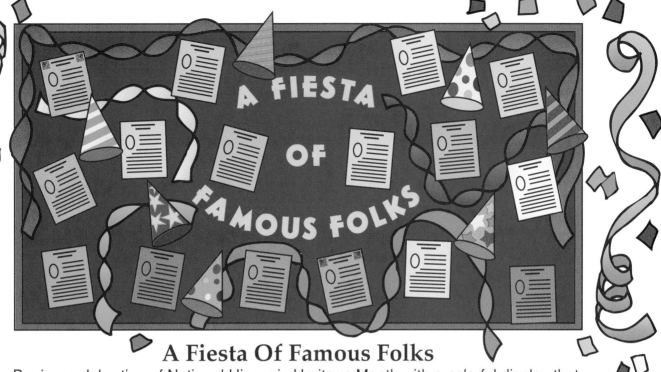

A Fiesta Of Famous Folks

Begin a celebration of National Hispanic Heritage Month with a colorful display that introduces students to notable Hispanic Americans. Add a title and real party streamers and hats to a board as shown. Next duplicate the resource list/certificate on page 93 on pastel colors of paper. Assign each student one notable person to research. Have the student use the information he finds to complete a certificate about the person. After presenting their findings to the class, ask students to cut out their certificates and attach them to the bulletin board.

Hispanic Influences All Around

Every region of our country is touched historically and culturally by Hispanic influences. From migrant farmers working the fields from which we get our food, to restaurants, architecture, and geographical names, we're reminded of these influences every day. Divide students into groups of three and send them on a scavenger hunt to investigate Hispanic contributions in your area and in their lives. Provide each group with a large, poster-size sheet of paper and the list of questions below. Have students decorate their paper with menus, pictures, news articles, and any other information they find as they try to answer these questions.

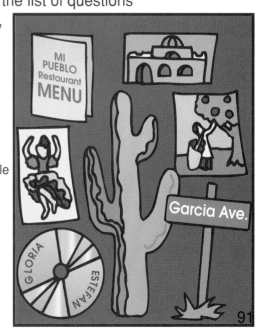

- Which Hispanic explorers, if any, visited our area of the country?
- Which homes and other buildings in our community were influenced by Spanish architecture?
- Is there a Mexican or other Hispanic restaurant in our area? Are there other restaurants in our area that serve Hispanic cuisine?
- Are there Spanish-language newspapers, magazines, and books available in our area?
- Are there farms in our area that rely on Hispanic migrant workers?
- Are there students of Hispanic heritage in our class or in our school?
- What names (of streets, towns, rivers, counties, etc.) in our community reflect a Hispanic influence?
- Do you listen to music performed by Americans of Hispanic descent (for example, Gloria Estefan)?
- What Hispanic TV actors, movie stars, or other entertainers have you seen?

Seeing Through Stereotypes

Present the following character descriptions to your students and ask them to identify each one:

- He wears thick glasses; reads every available minute; seldom acknowledges others, even when spoken to.
- She gets up early each morning and jogs; eats fruit and wheat germ for breakfast; plays tennis at lunch.
- She wears lots of expensive jewels and furs; poses constantly as if a photographer is catching her every move.
- He sits in a rocking chair; can't hear very well; often talks about the past.

More than likely, students identified a bookworm, a health nut, a movie star, and an elderly person. Television shows, movies, and books often deal with one-sided characters, or *stereotypes.* Ask students to define *stereotype* (a person considered typical of a kind and without individuality). Hispanic Americans, like other ethnic groups, are often subject to injustices and prejudice due to unfair stereotypes. Ask students if they have seen or heard stereotypical comments about Hispanic Americans, or about any ethnic group. Ask students how they feel about stereotypes: "Are stereotypes accurate? Harmful? Funny? Demeaning?" Also discuss what happens when people rely on stereotypes to form opinions.

Follow up this discussion by asking students to list stereotypes that they see in TV shows and commercials over a seven-day period. Instruct students to describe the attributes of these characters and explain why they are stereotypical. Provide time for students to discuss what they saw; then lead them to conclude that it's unfair and inaccurate to judge people by stereotypes, and that it's important to know when a stereotyped character is being presented.

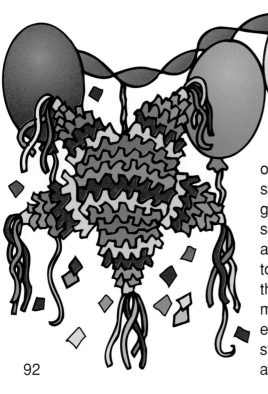

Let's Have A Fiesta!

What's more fun than a party? Celebrate the conclusion of your Hispanic Heritage Month activities with a fiesta that students plan themselves. Divide your class into six groups. Provide each group with a copy of the planning sheet on page 94. Have each group elect a chairperson and a recorder; then allot about 30 minutes for each group to meet and fill out all sections of the sheet. At the end of the planning stage, discuss the fiesta with the entire class, making sure that you will have a good variety of food and entertainment (sections I and III). Provide about a week for students to prepare for the party. Then get ready to enjoy a fiesta your class will remember forever!

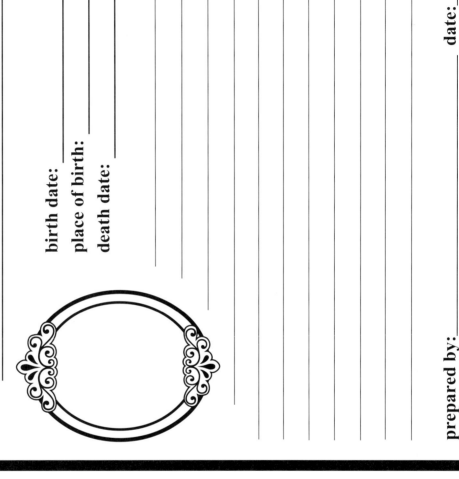

Focusing On A
Famous Hispanic American

This certificate honors:

birth date:

place of birth:

death date:

prepared by: _____ date: _____

Notable Hispanic Americans

Entertainment
Desi Arnaz
Joan Baez
Rubén Blades
Gloria Estefan
Emilio Estévez
Andy García
José Arcadia Limón
Rita Moreno
Lou Diamond Phillips
Geraldo Rivera
Linda Ronstadt
Charlie Sheen
Martin Sheen
Jimmy Smits
Ritchie Valens

Sports
José Canseco
Michael Carbajal
Roberto Clemente
Tom Flores
Richard "Pancho" Gonzales
Nancy Lopez
Max Montoya
Jim Plunkett
Lou Piniella
Chi Chi Rodriguez
Ruben Sierra
Jose Torres
Lee Trevino
Fernando Valenzuela

Education
Lauro Cavazos
Jaime Escalante
Richard Rodriquez
Adelina Otero Warren

Government/Civil Rights
César Chávez
Henry Cisneros
Dennis Chávez
Henry Barbosa Gonzales
Lena Guerrero
Manuel Lujan
Vilma S. Martínez
Katherine Davalos Ortega

Fine Arts/Literature
Fernando Bujones
Pablo Casals
Carlos Castenada
Evelyn Cisneros
Oscar Hijuelos
Marisol
George Santayana
Luis Valdes

Science/Medicine
Luis Alvarez
Dr. Antonia C. Novello
Dr. Ellen Ochoa
Dr. Severo Ochoa

Note To The Teacher: Use this reproducible with "A Fiesta Of Famous Folks" on page 91. Have the student draw a picture of his famous person in the oval frame.

Fiesta!

Celebrating National Hispanic Heritage Month
Group Planning Sheet

Group members: _____

_____

Chairperson: _____ Recorder:_____

Date of our fiesta: _____ Number of students in our class: _____

I. **Food (for the entire class)**
   Our group will bring (circle two choices):
   a. an ethnic food
   b. a vegetable
   c. a fruit
   d. drinks
   e. a dessert
   f. other: _____

II. **Decorations**
   Our group will bring or make: _____

   _____

   _____

III. **Entertainment**
   Our group will (circle two choices):
   a. write and perform a skit about a historical event related to National Hispanic Heritage Month
   b. sing a traditional Hispanic song
   c. perform a traditional Hispanic dance
   d. bring music by Hispanic performers
   e. write and present at least three famous Hispanic American interviews
   f. teach a Hispanic-related craft to the class
   g. dramatize and present a Hispanic folktale or short story

IV. **Materials we need to gather** _____

   _____

V. **People we can call on to help us** _____

   _____

VI. **Resources that will help us** _____

   _____

Note To The Teacher: Use this reproducible with "Let's Have A Fiesta!" on page 92.

Answer Keys

Bonus Box answer: There is a total of 55 squares in the grid:

25 squares that are 1 x 1   4 squares that are 4 x 4
16 squares that are 2 x 2   1 square that is 5 x 5
9 squares that are 3 x 3

Page 71
Bonus Box answer: John Adams was in England serving as ambassador. Thomas Jefferson was our ambassador to France.

Page 73

Part 1: Read each clue. In the first blank, write the name of the state. In the second blank, write its number on the map.

a. I sent no delegates to the convention. I was the last of the 13 states to approve the Constitution.
   Rhode Island   13

b. The Constitutional Convention was held in one of my cities. Ben Franklin was one of my most famous residents. Pennsylvania   2

c. A famous compromise made between the big and little states was named for me. I was the fifth state to approve the Constitution. Connecticut   5

d. I was the smallest state to attend the Convention. I was first to approve the Constitution.
   Delaware   1

e. George Washington and James Madison both served as my delegates.
   Virginia   10

f. I led the small states with a plan (named for me). It called for equal representation in both the Senate and the House. New Jersey   3

g. The Constitution was ratified when I voted *yes* on June 21, 1788.
   New Hampshire   9

h. I was the southernmost state and was fourth to approve the Constitution.
   Georgia   4

i. I am an agricultural state that depended on slavery. I first voted *no*, but changed my mind later and voted *yes*. North Carolina   12

j. My delegates included Charles Pinckney and his cousin, also named Charles Pinckney! I voted *yes* on May 23, 1788. South Carolina   8

k. I am sandwiched between Virginia and Pennsylvania. I approved the Constitution on April 28, 1788.
   Maryland   7

l. I am home to Plymouth Rock. I approved the Constitution on February 6, 1788.
   Massachusetts   6

m. Alexander Hamilton was my delegate after John Lansing, Jr., and Robert Yates walked out. New York   11

Part 2: Color blue the states that approved the Constitution before it was ratified. Color yellow the states that approved the Constitution after it had been ratified.

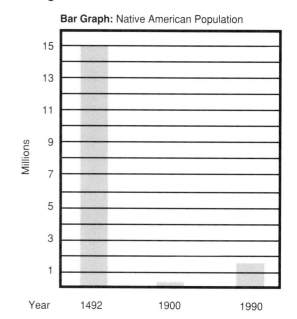

Dates of Ratification			
Map No.	Date	Map No.	Date
1	12/7/1787	8	5/23/1788
2	12/12/1787	9	6/21/1788
3	12/18/1787	10	6/25/1788
4	1/2/1788	11	7/26/1788
5	1/9/1788	12	11/21/1789
6	2/6/1788	13	5/29/1790
7	4/28/1788		

Page 85

Bar Graph: Native American Population

Line Graph: Native American Population

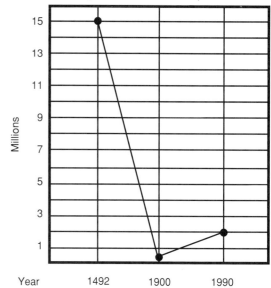

Pictograph: Native American Population

1492	●●●●●●●●●●●●●●●
1900	◢
1990	●●

KEY ● = 1,000,000 Native Americans

95

Answer Keys

Page 87

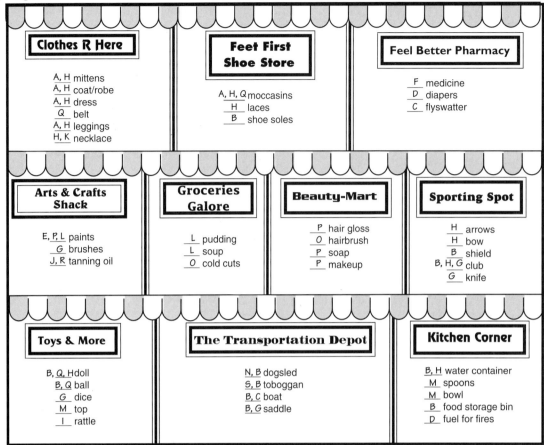

Clothes R Here

A, H mittens
A, H coat/robe
A, H dress
Q belt
A, H leggings
H, K necklace

Feet First Shoe Store

A, H, Q moccasins
H laces
B shoe soles

Feel Better Pharmacy

F medicine
D diapers
C flyswatter

Arts & Crafts Shack

E, P, L paints
G brushes
J, R tanning oil

Groceries Galore

L pudding
L soup
O cold cuts

Beauty-Mart

P hair gloss
O hairbrush
P soap
P makeup

Sporting Spot

H arrows
H bow
B shield
B, H, G club
G knife

Toys & More

B, Q, H doll
B, Q ball
G dice
M top
I rattle

The Transportation Depot

N, B dogsled
S, B toboggan
B, C boat
B, G saddle

Kitchen Corner

B, H water container
M spoons
M bowl
B food storage bin
D fuel for fires

Additional information:

- Thread—used to sew items such as clothing and moccasins—was made from tendons taken from the buffalo.
- Dolls were made with soft hide and stuffed with buffalo hair. Stick dolls were held together with thongs made from tendons.
- Boats were kept from spinning by leaving the tail of the buffalo on the hide, attaching a piece of wood to it, and suspending it from the back of the boat.
- A ball was made of buffalo hide filled with hair.
- Buffalo tongues were dried whole, then sliced to make food similar to our cold cuts.
- To make a hairbrush, the top, rough side of the tongue was dried in an arch shape, with the tongue ridges raised to make the brush's "teeth."
- The buffalo's tail was fastened to a stick to make a flyswatter.
- Dried buffalo dung, called *buffalo chips,* burned with a hot, clear fire. They were a readily available form of fuel that stayed dry even after a rain.
- Dried buffalo dung that was pounded to a fine powder was used as disposable diapers for babies. After a baby was placed inside a cradleboard, the powder was poured around the baby from the waist down. It kept the infant's skin from being irritated. When the baby needed to be changed, the soiled dung powder was thrown away and replaced with new powder.
- The heart was the one part of the buffalo that wasn't used. Native Americans left the heart on the plains, believing that it served as "seed" for new herds.

Page 88

Some answers may vary.
1. deerskin; the tribe probably killed deer for food and other supplies. They were hunters.
2. A-3, B-3, C-3; these Native Americans made masks, probably for religious ceremonies. Corn was available for making masks.
3. the area located around the coordinates A-1, B-1, and C-1; berries, corn, fish. This indicates they did some farming and fishing, and that they were located near a body of water.
4. deerskin; the deerskin and the deerskin moccasins
5. probably; wampum was found at the site.